THE MAN IN THE ARENA

Four true stroies from the standup
comedian turned adventure travel writer

Joel Paul Reisig

"Best wishes as you continue your adventures." -Robert Redford

The author would like to thank: Brian McKeever, his family, and his crew, Gary Lafew and the Muxlow brothers, Joshua 9-Fingers, my first boxing coach Joe Kahne, and my partents - Marty and Julie Reisig.

CONTENTS

"It is not the critic who counts; not the man who points out how the strong man stumbles, or where the doer of deeds could have done them better. The credit belongs to the man who is actually in the arena, whose face is marred by dust and sweat and blood; who strives valiantly; who errs, who comes short again and again, because there is no effort without error and shortcoming; but who does actually strive to do the deeds; who knows great enthusiasms, the great devotions; who spends himself in a worthy cause; who at the best knows in the end the triumph of high achievement, and who at the worst, if he fails, at least fails while daring greatly, so that his place shall never be with those cold and timid souls who neither know victory nor defeat."

-Theodore Roosevelt, 26th president of the United States

DEMOLITION DERBY

"Unlike a football game, there is no ground to take, no points to score. There is only mayhem and survival."

There are a handful of staples that can always be found at the county fair. The Ferris Wheel, the Merry-Go-Round, the haunted house.

None hold the interest of kids as much as bumper cars. Not even the shooting gallery, or the tattooed ex con hitting on the high school girls. Nothing compares to getting to drive. The only thing better than driving? Smashing!

According to the Showmen's Museum in Miami, the Stoehrer brothers were the first to patent their bumper cars when they created the Dodgem Company. Their first patent was filed in December 1920. Originally, the rides really were a parent's nightmare. Made of tin, the cars sometimes had to be nailed back together between rides. They could be dented with one good kick. Sometimes parts came off during the ride. The Scientific American deemed them "unmanageable." Yet a hundred years later the bumper cars are still around, and kids at fairs everywhere still love them.

What could be more fun than a kid's game of bumper cars? How about twenty fully grown idiots smashing full sized real American steel cars into each other with as much force as they could muster! Today I was packing up my college diploma and heading south to become one of those idiots.

Around 11:30 pm I rolled into Mount Vernon, Ohio. A few minutes later I pulled into Brian McKeever's driveway.

I had been talking to Brian online for a couple of weeks now. By all accounts he seemed like a very normal guy. He had a wife, a new born son, a house, and a job with the city. His only eccentricity, on weekends he crashes cars.

Brian was the de facto leader of B 12 Racing, a group of buddies who built derby cars, watched each other's kids, helped each other out when needed with the phase "you'll pay me back later", stood in each other's weddings, and went to the country fairs together to compete in demolition derbies.

His garage was their clubhouse, a tree fort for adults. "A derby lasts maybe fifteen minutes", Brian would later tell me, "but most cars will be out in three to five. Running the derby is a bonus; it's just an excuse to be able to do what we do all summer. It's a reason for the guys to come over and hang out."

He was a pleasant guy, mid 20s, about my height but heavy, around 250 lbs. Did that help for the sport? Add a little heft to each of your hits? I decided to sleep first and ask later. He wore clean clothes, standard jeans and T shirt from Walmart, not dirty but not trying to impress anybody either. I liked him from the start.

Brian showed me to a comfortable room in the basement; I blew up my air mattress and crawled right into bed. "You got everything you need?" Brian asked me.

"Yeah, perfect. Thanks for having me."

"No problem. I'm just going to ask you one favor."

"Sure"

"Whenever I see a documentary on demolition derby, they always make us out to be a bunch of hillbillies. They follow around some toothless redneck because, hey, that's what gets ratings. I just hope you won't do that."

"I'm going to write the truth, whatever I see."

"Thanks."

"Goodnight bud."

Like I normally do, I lay in an unusual room wondering how I had gotten myself here, and what the hell had I gotten myself into?

As the hours ticked off, I googled and read about demolition derbies.

Demolition derby is a motorsport usually presented at county fairs and festivals. While rules vary from event to event, the typical demolition derby event consists of twenty drivers competing by deliberately ramming their vehicles into one another. The last driver whose vehicle is still operational is awarded the victory.

Demolition derbies originated in the United States and quickly spread to other Western nations. First held at various fairs, race tracks, and speedways by independent promoters in the 1950s, there are unconfirmed reports of events occurring as far back as the 1930s utilizing the abundant supply of worn-out Ford Model Ts.

The originator of the concept for auto demolition derbies is disputed. One source says that Don Basile is often credited with inventing the demolition derby at Carrell Speedway in 1947. The best creation myth of demolition derby dates to 1958, when Long Island stock-car driver Lawrence Mendelsohn flipped his '49 Ford at the New York State Islip Speedway and sailed 12 rows up into an empty grandstand. While he was suspended upside-down in his car Mendelsohn watched the crowd go nuts on the far side of the track. As time slowed down for him, he realized, prior to landing on his head, that folks were really paying to see the crashes.

A true history of the birth of demolition derby must trace all the way back to the public destruction of cars in the form of automotive thrill shows, the so-called "Hell Drivers" who traveled the country in circus-like troupes in the early 1920s. These dare devil drivers were known for leaping obsolete vehicles through rings of flame, or simply crashing them headlong into each other as ecstatic small-town audiences roared their approval.

The sport's popularity grew throughout the 1960s, becoming a standard at county fairs and a new subculture nationwide. The popularity of demolition derbies also spread overseas. In 1963 a reported crowd of 20,000 packed into the Rowley Park Speedway in Adelaide to see Australia's first demolition derby. Due to the size of the crowd (about twice the venue capacity), the police closed the speedway's gates. The derby itself had over 75 entries and lasted for over 100 minutes

The sport's popularity peaked in the 1970s. ABC's Wide World of Sports televised the World Championship Demolition Derby from the mid-1960s until 1992. In 1972, the Los Angeles Coliseum hosted a demolition derby with mint-condition late model cars.

Still around in the modern century, in 2001, the Los Angeles Times estimated that between 60,000 and 75,000 drivers participated in at least one of the 2,000 demolition derbies held in the United States that year. More recently promoter Tory Schutte of Genoa City, Wisconsin estimated about 5,000 derbies are held each year at county fairs nationwide.

Demolition derbies can be dangerous. Although serious injuries are rare, they do happen.

It's not always the drivers who are at risk. In 2019 a woman was killed, and at least seven others were injured, when a car competing at a demolition derby in Montana drove over a chain-link fence into spectators, authorities said.

In the morning I got to know Brian, and I got to meet the rest of the gang.

I have to admit that Brian was surprisingly articulate, intelligent, and educated. He was basically a suburban kid who happened to live in the middle of nowhere. It just wasn't the mental picture I had. I believe I had expected a guy who was married to his second cousin and constantly yelling at his fourteen-year-old boy for drinkin' all his gosh damn beer again. If anything, Brian reminded me of the many great guys I met while attending Hope College.

Brittney, Brian's wife, had no problem with me being there for the long weekend and treated me like a cousin who was coming to visit. (And no, not the kind of cousin that I was just talking about).

Sean was Brian's best friend, another super nice guy who drove truck for a living. He did not drive "a truck". I noticed that, like all truck drivers, he for some reason skipped the "a" and constantly said "I drive truck". I didn't ask his age, but like Brian he appeared to be just under thirty. Also like Brian, if I'm being honest, he didn't skip any meals.

Sean's wife, Ashley, was friends with both Brian and Brian's wife Brittney. She too spent a lot of time at the house, taking photos, watching kids, and generally hanging out and enjoying the summer days and weeks.

Adam had his own set of keys to Brian's house, and although I never went upstairs, I think he had his own room too. A nice guy who worked at McDonalds. He just wanted a good group of guys to hang around. Don't we all?

In his garage Brian did not build demolition derby cars, he created a family. I was reminded of my favorite book when I was a kid, <u>The Outsiders</u> by SE Hinton. It was a gang story, full of gang fights, but the boys in the book were not a gang, they were just buddies. People bond like this all across the country, all across the world I'm sure. Motorcycle clubs, Elk's and Moose lodges, the regulars at your neighborhood bar, the old guys in the Belgium Feather Bowling club in Detroit, and groups that wear neon color spandex and go bike riding. We all just want a good group of guys to hang out with.

Often people drive through expensive neighborhoods and are envious of the large houses. I understand. I've done it myself. But just because a house looks nice from the outside does not mean that nice things are happening inside. The truth is many of those homes are occupied by a man who works too much, a wife who lives in a separate bedroom and takes too many pills, and one single child who hates them both and does whatever she wants. Not many people would drive by Brian's house, a middle-class home with an extra-large garage in a very rural neighborhood, and feel envy. But they should. Brian had a tribe.

Two other guys popped in and out. I called them Doofus and Dipstick.

If Brian represented the extreme opposite of what you would expect from a stereotypical demolition derby driver, these two were Hollywood cast to play the roles. Camouflage hats, muddy boots, T shirts with big armpit holes, and chewing tobacco constantly in their mouths. They pulled up two lawn chairs and remained there for the rest of the weekend, drinking cheap beer while the other guys worked.

Brian looked at Doofus and Dipstick, then he looked at me, then he looked back at them as if seeing them for the very first time in his life. I could see the wheels turning in Brian's head as he imagined the words that would appear on my page. I think he thought about saying something, something along the lines of how atypical they were in the sport, but changed his mind and instead changed the subject to the real subject, cars.

"Want to have a look at your car?"

"Absolutely."

He opened the garage and revealed a 1983 Cadillac, painted purple and rust, exhaust pipes coming through the hood, radiator smashed backwards into the engine, the entire rear end of the car crunched up and falling off, and huge mud tires.

"That's some Mad Max shit right there." I smiled.

"I wouldn't put you in it if it wasn't safe." Brian assured me.

"It don't look like much but it run good!" Doofus laughed.

"It doesn't look like much but it runs well." Brian quietly said to me.

"It looks perfect." I told him.

"We'll get the front end pulled out and the radiator fixed. The back looks terrible but we'll fold it up and wire it in place, it actually makes for a good rear end pad. The frame of the car is still strong in the front so I'd suggest hitting head on mostly; just use reverse to get yourself out of trouble."

"Sounds good."

"And most of all we'll add anything you want for safety. You'll be driving in the 80s stock class and there are pretty strict rules about the modifications you can make to your car, but they let you do anything you want for driver's side safety. "

"Perfect."

"Let's go to work."

"Let's go to breakfast."

"Even better."

Brian, Sean, Adam and I went into Mount Vernon to get some food.

Mount Vernon, Ohio, was founded in 1805 and named after the estate of George Washington. Today it has seventeen thousand people, two universities, and, believe it or not, the oldest surviving opera house in the United States.

Mount Vernon was also the home of Johnathon Chapman, better know as Johnny Appleseed.

Chapman (September 26, 1774 – March 18, 1845), was an American pioneer nurseryman who introduced apple trees to large parts of Pennsylvania, Ontario, Ohio, Indiana, and Illinois, as well as the northern counties of present-day West Virginia. He became an American legend while still alive, due to his kind generous ways, and his leadership in conservation.

One cool autumnal night, as the story goes, Chapman while lying by his camp-fire in the woods, observed that the mosquitoes flew in the blaze and were burned. Johnny, who wore on his head a tin utensil which answered both as a cap and a mush pot, filled it with water and quenched the fire, and afterwards remarked, "God forbid that I should build a fire for my comfort, that should be the means of destroying any of His creatures.

A vegetarian, the Native Americans regarded him as someone who had been touched by the Great Spirit, and even hostile tribes left him strictly alone.

Today the Fort Wayne TinCaps, a minor league baseball team in Fort Wayne, Indiana, where Chapman spent his final years, is named in Johnny Appleseed's honor. Or perhaps to mock him for wearing a tin bowl on his head? One of the two.

"I'm thinking Big Boys!" Adam yelled from the back seat of the truck. Like Brian and Sean, he wasn't exactly on a diet. Break out a pair of checkered overalls and any of them could have stood in front of a Big Boys.

"I'm sure he has Big Boy's in Michigan. Joel wants to see somewhere local."

"I'd rather, if its fine with you guys."

"This is your weekend bud." Brian told me. "We just want you to have a good time. Sean, go to Southside."

The Southside Diner was a local fifties style diner. The booths were bright and the walls were full of Elvis, Marilyn Monroe, James Dean, winter sleds, and classic bicycles. A jukebox was stuffed into every corner. I liked it.

"What can I get for you boys?"

"I'll take the Gus Buster." The Gus Buster was three eggs, hash browns, pancakes, bacon, and sausage.

"Anything else for you honey?"

"No, no I believe the three eggs, pancakes, hash browns, bacon, and sausage will hold me over till lunch. Just one question though, who was Gus?

"Gus Bizos. He used to order that every day." Gus apparently was also not on a diet. I suppose I wasn't either.

In the end I could not bust the Gus Buster. A take home box was in order.

"I got the check." Brian told me.

"Nope, I'll take that." I paid for the check and Brian thanked me about three times.

"Brian's not used to anyone doing anything nice for him." Sean told me.

"That's not true."

"Yes it is. He gives and gives and most guys just take and take. He's the nicest guy I know, but some guys will take advantage of it."

"Thanks again for breakfast, Joel."

"Brian you're letting me stay at your house, teaching me about derbies, and letting me smash up one of your cars. "

"Oh, well, none of that's a big deal."

In the afternoon we started working on the car. I quickly

learned two things. One, working on older model American cars is exponentially easier than new foreign cars! There's tons of room to work, the parts are all large and you can figure out what they do; it just wasn't nearly as complicated as I had expected.

By the mid-1980s, oil prices had fallen sharply, helping lead to the revitalization of the American auto industry. Sometimes referred to as "Yank Tanks," traditional full-size 1980s American sedans are as much a part of U.S. culture as apple pie and baseball.

Large cars that took up two parallel parking spaces, gangsters could fit three or four bodies in the trunk, room for a good-sized boy to lay out flat without a seat belt and sleep while his father smoked and roared down the interstate at 75 mph. These were American cars. With curb weights over four thousand pounds they could smash through anything that got in their way. I was counting on it.

The second thing I learned was this; building a demolition car is just a bunch of guys brain storming, then taking the best idea. Adam suggested that we fill the driver's side door with cement, so we did. It was the first time the guys had done that. Even some of my ideas were accepted and used.

Brian's dad stopped by in the afternoon.
"So you're going to run in the derby?"
"I am."
He looked at my car. "In that?"
About ten minutes after he left, Sean's grandpa came over. He gave my car a once over, "Well there ain't much left to that one, is there?"
I looked at the car again. I only had two fears going into this weekend. First, I was afraid that I would get too amt up and slam into another guy's driver side door, injuring him. My second fear was mismatched cars. I did not want to be in an event where I was at a major advantage or disadvantage before we even started. It wouldn't be fun, and it would be a safety risk.
As if reading my mind, Brian said "We'll make it safe."
"So you boys been workin'?" Sean's grandpa asked us.

"A little bit."

"A good day of demolition derby work lasts ten hours. You got yourself two hours of work, and eight hours of bullshitting!"

When he left, we got back to work. That afternoon I pounded out the frame with a sledge hammer, learned to change an exhaust system, did a very subpar job on my first-time welding, did an equally lousy job with the cutting torch, mixed cement and dumped it into the driver's side door, and jacked up the rear end so we could wire it into place.

"So what goes on here at night?"

"Fox Hole!" Doofus smiled.

"What's that?"

"Strip club."

"Ah. What else is around?"

"Nothing really. Couple of bars and the college."

"College? There you go. Why don't we go to a college party?"

"Cause I don't want to get my ass kicked."

"Why would you get your ass kicked?"

"Don't belong. Last time me and Dipstick went there they just about kicked our asses."

I could see what Doofus meant. He had a huge gut that his old T shirt didn't quite cover, sleeves cut off to reveal tattooed arms, beard, trucker hat, and Walmart work clothes. Dipstick was skinny as a twig, had a scraggly excuse for a mustache, bangs and a mullet. I could blend into any college in America, but they could not.

"I went to college for three weeks!" Dipstick told me.

"I went for two weeks!" Doofus smiled.

"Guys, please don't brag about that." Brian again looked at me with the "most demolition drivers are really normal" look.

"I'm not that into strip clubs." I told them.

"It's real shitty anyway." Adam told me. "Just a hole in the wall joint with a bunch of ugly girls."

"You got to bring your own beer." Doofus chimed in.

"Well if we do go make sure you text me." Sean said as he

climbed into his truck. "My grandpa's been wanting to go."

"Whoa, whoa, whoa! Slow down!" I laughed. "You're telling me that you have a locally operated, hole in the wall, two-dollar strip club, with a bunch of lunch ladies dancing, and it's BYOB?"

"Haha, yep!"

"And your grandfather wants to come with us?"

"Yeah, I don't suppose you'd want to write about any of that."

"It's exactly what I want to write about. We're going."

"You guys have fun." Brian said. "I'm married. I've never been to one anyway. But I don't go to bars either 'cause I don't drink. I'll probably just watch a little TV and go to sleep."

"Alright. You want me to stay over at Adam or Sean's tonight, so I don't wake you?"

"I'm staying here." Adam said.

"You guys won't wake us. Adam has a key."

Sean drove Adam and me, in Brian's truck, to the Fox Hole. As we drove, the guys told me a really interesting story. New Castle, Ohio has two main attractions, a very small strip club, and a very small church. As you might imagine, both of these establishments would like to see the other run out of town.

Every Friday night for the past eight years New Beginnings Ministries holds a protest outside of the Fox Hole strip club. Residents say the protesters can be heard through locked doors and closed windows a full three hundred yards away.

Kelly Wilson said friends refuse to visit on Fridays because of the situation, and she said she and her husband can't even watch television in peace. Another resident complained that her teenage son can't walk home from work at Peggy Sue's Steak and Ribs without being heckled by protesters.

It does not appear that The Fox Hole has lost any business due to the protesters, but that hasn't stopped them from striking back. They figured that what is good for the goose is good for the gander, so they decided to hold their own protests. Every Sunday morning, they protest in front of the church, topless. According to Ohio revised code, the topless protests are legal.

I have to wonder if perhaps church attendance has gone up?

I must say, The Fox Hole was everything I had hoped it would be. The building was an old tin box that used to be a gas station. Converted to a strip club in 1999, it was roughly a fifteen by thirty foot falling down old building with worn out lettering on the outside. I didn't really believe any of the guys, but it actually was BYOB. There were no bouncers, none, not even a middle-aged fat guy. I couldn't believe it, a strip club inside of an old gas station, that allowed you to bring, and drink, as much as you wanted, without a single bouncer! How the hell was this place possible?

There was only one thing that truly disappointed me, the girls were not half as ugly as promised. In fact, six of them were marginally attractive while the other two, both around nineteen years old, were nothing short of stunning.

"Damn." Sean mumbled. "They brought out their A game for Memorial Day weekend."

We paid our twelve dollar covers, got our change in singles, and found a place to sit. There were only three rows of seating, the tip rail, one row of tables that would seat a total of maybe ten people, and a bench in the back that could hold another eight or so.

The club was filled with exactly the type of guys that Brian was hoping I wouldn't see all weekend. They all looked the same, work boots, Walmart jeans, old T shirts with oil stains on them, extremely short haircuts that they either did themselves or had their buddies do, and a trucker hat. There were also two old rock and roll burn outs, a couple of fat lesbians, and a pack of young skinny bikers with goofy vests. I was truly disappointed to learn that Sean's grandpa would not be able to join us.

I sat back and watched a fat guy throw a wad of about twenty or so singles into the air. I know that conventional wisdom says that strip clubs are bad because they are objectifying women. This may be true and one could argue the point, but are they not also taking advantage of men? Are men not really the ones who are suffering here? I am completely serious as I ask this question. I watched guy after guy throwing money, money that they really couldn't afford, onto the stage just so they could buy another minute of the fantasy. A fantasy of a life that he will never have.

"We got beer!" Doofus and Dipstick yelled as they walked in with a couple cases of the cheapest beer possible. Then Dipstick continued to yell, "Look at them nice titties! Them is some nice titties!" The music stopped halfway through his sentence but he did not adjust the volume of his voice. Sean slunk down a bit in his seat, embarrassed to be seen with them.

Dipstick took a seat at the tip rail. When the girl came around and danced for him he put a five dollar bill in her G string. He then made change by removing four of the singles that were already in there.

"So you're going to run derby?" Doofus asked me.

"That's the idea."

"What are you doing?" Asked one of the two really good looking nineteen-year-old girls. Cali sat down at our table and introduced herself.

"He's going to run one of our cars in the demolition derby."

"He gonna get all fucked up!" Dipstick yelled from the tip rail.

"Shut up Dipstick." Sean yelled back at him.

"You're not from around here, are you?" Cali asked me.

"What gave me away?"

"Everything."

"He's an adventure travel writer." Adam told her.

"What's that mean?"

So Cali and I talked for the next two hours. I know this sounds weird, but she was pretty great. She was studying to be a vet tech, had an amazing smile, honestly the whole thing just felt like I was back at a college party, in a crowded basement but totally alone with the prettiest girl in the house. That fantasy was of course interrupted every thirty minutes when she went on stage to show everyone else her tits, but other than that it was pretty great.

Now I am aware of the classic argument: strippers only pretend to like you to get your money, but over the course of two hours I gave her roughly four dollars, sitting at the tip rail while she danced, then we went back to standing in the back of the club, just the two of us, no money changing hands. At the end of the night she gave me one of my dollars back, with her phone number written on it.

"Did she just tip you!" Adam yelled. "How the hell does that work???"

"Adam!" Sean quickly picked up on what was happening. If she was seen giving me her number she would probably get fired. "Shut up."

I shoved the dollar in my pocket and we kept talking for another half hour.

"Alright boys!" Doofus yelled. "We're taking off."

"Let me drive you." Sean said to them. He drove a truck for a living, something that he took very seriously. He knew that he was going to drive Adam and me home tonight so he hadn't had a single beer all night.

"I'm alright!" Doofus grinned, showing off a few missing teeth.

"You're drunk out of your mind Doofus."

"Then he'll drive." He gave the keys to Dipstick.

"I'm a professional drunk driver!" Dipstick laughed and the two of them ran out the door before Sean could say anything else.

"You're looking for love."

"Huh?" I turned around and saw a fat-woman looking at me. Behind her sat her husband, laughing.

"You."

"What about me?"

"You're looking for love. I've been watching you."

"Ok."

"Your dad's a dentist."

"I don't follow."

"He is. I know it."

"He's not."

"He is. Look at them teeth."

"Ah, I see. That would be an orthodontist, but he's not."

"Oreo what? I don't know what that is."

"I can see that."

"You're hot."

"Thank you, that's very nice of you to say."

"You want to go out to the truck?"

"Um, no, no, I'm good right here."

"Go on!" Her husband yelled. "Doing me a favor!"

"That's very nice of both of you, thank you, but I'm ok."

"What are you, a fucking fag?" Her husband yelled at me.

I assumed I was now going to have to punch out a drunk, and possibly also her husband, but she just said "Whatever", and walked away.

Cali laughed; she had been standing there the whole time.

"You heard that?"

"Oh yeah, she liked you!"

"You could have saved me."

"Now where would the fun be in that? She probably would have given you twenty dollars." She laughed.

"I wasn't very into her."

"I know the feeling."

"Yeah."

"Are you really going to text me and let me be in the pits with you at the demolition derby?" Cali asked me.

"Sure."

"You know if I don't hear from you, I'm going to be sad. I mean it."

"I'll see you on Monday."

"Ok."

Adam slept in the back seat as Sean drove Brian's truck home.

"Dang." Sean said.

"What's up?"

"I don't know how I'm going to explain to my wife that I spent sixty bucks at the strip club."

"She doesn't know that you went?"

"No, she knows, she's cool about stuff like that. She just isn't going to be happy that I spent sixty bucks there. I'm going to need to figure out something to tell her."

"Ok, so you spent twelve dollars on the cover to get in, you gave me your eight dollars change in singles just to be a nice guy and make sure I had a good time, and then you put forty dollars of gas into Brian's truck."

Sean sat there with a blank look on his face for about thirty seconds. "Dang, you're really good with math. She'll buy that, cause it's all complicated so it sounds true."

"No problem."

"No, I better just tell her the truth."

"Ok."

We rode in silence for awhile. After five minutes I woke, without noticing that I had been sleeping. I told Sean that I was sorry.

"What for?"

"I fell asleep for a minute there. I meant to stay up and talk with you."

"That's alright; I'm used to driving alone anyway. I log about 3,200 miles a week."

"Wow."

"It's a good job. I put 2,000 dollars in my bank every week. Ashley is a stay-at-home mom, and we have three kids. How old do you think I am?"

"30?"

"45."

"Shut up. You are not." He was overweight, but other than that he would be the most youthful looking 45 I had ever seen.

"I was born in 1981."

"Ok, that's 35, not 45."

"No, it's 45."

"It's not."

"Wait, but I'm really 25 and I took ten years off of my real birth date."

"Right, so 25 plus the ten years is 35. If you wanted to pretend to be 45 you would have had to have said 1971."

"Dang. You really are good at math." We rode in silence for a while more.

America's trucking industry is the lifeblood of the U.S. economy. In fact, nearly every good consumed in the U.S. is put on a truck at some point. The trucking industry hauled 72.5% of all freight transported in the United States in 2019, equating to 11.84 billion tons.

If trucks were stopped for twenty- four hours hospitals would run out of basic supplies, U.S. mail and other package delivery would cease within one day, food shortages would begin to develop, and automobile fuel would dwindle, leading to high prices and long lines at gas pumps. All of these conditions would happen if trucks were only stopped for a mere twenty-four hours.

In two to three days, conditions would escalate even further. If trucks were stopped for just a few days service stations would completely run out of fuel, ATM's would run out of cash and banks would be unable to process transactions, supplies of essential food and water would disappear, and garbage would start piling up in urban and suburban areas.

By the 4th week of trucks stopping, the nation's clean water supply would be completely exhausted.

A lot of people hate sharing the road with trucks, but the truth is we cars are not sharing our road with trucks; the trucks are sharing their road with us. If the trucks were to stop rolling, America would quickly fail.

"That part about driving 3,200 miles a week. Was that true?"

"Yeah. It's a good paying job, but it gets real lonely. You know there are hookers at every truck stop?"

"Doesn't surprise me."

"I've never cheated on my wife. Closest I've ever come is The Fox Hole just looking at some tits, but that's nothing and we hardly ever go there. Now I did some stuff before I was married that I'm not proud of, but not after."

"Ok."

"But man its lonesome. Sometimes I'll tell a girl, I'll tell her, I don't want nothing sexual but I'll give you ten bucks just to talk to me for awhile. Sometimes I'll talk to them, see if I can get them out of it. A lot of them aren't even 18."

Child prostitution usually manifests in the form of sex trafficking, in which a child is kidnapped, or more often tricked, into becoming involved in the sex trade, or survival sex, in which the child engages in sexual activities to procure basic essentials such as food and shelter.

There have been many attempts to estimate the number of juvenile prostitutes within the United States. As you can understand, it is impossible to ever take an accurate survey of the situation. These estimates range from 1,400 to 2.4 million, although most fall between 300,000 and 600,000.

We drove another ten miles or so down the county road. Adam snored in the back.

"I've asked Brian a few times how much money I should give him for this." I told Sean, "He just says 'don't worry about it'".

"He won't take anything from you. Brian's the nicest guy I know. He gets taken advantage of a lot because of it, and he knows it, but he just keeps right on being nice."

"That's why I'm asking you."

Sean thought about it for a moment. "I gave him two hundred dollars to run one of his cars in a derby. That seemed fair. But I don't think he'll take money from you. He just wants you to have a good time."

In the back, Adam woke up. "Hey Joel?"

"Yeah?"

"How the hell did you get that stripper to give you her number?"

"I talked to her like she was a person."

I reached into my pocket for the dollar bill. I had promised Cali I would text her later tonight, when we made it home safely, may as well do it now while we were still driving, I wanted to go to sleep as soon as I got home.

"Ah come on!" I yelled! Sean and Adam both looked at me.

"What?"

"I tipped her with it!"

"What?"

"The dollar bill that Cali wrote her number on. I had it in this pocket. I must have given it back to her the last time that she was on stage."

The guys laughed hysterically.

"You know for a college boy you sure are one dumb son of a bitch!"

"Where are Doofus and Dipstick this morning?" I asked. Brian, Adam, Sean, and I were out in the garage; it was around 11 am.

"Hung over. We won't see them today."

We got to work on the car. First up was changing the exhaust pipes. Brian handed me a wrench, told me what to do, and I got on it. While we worked, we bullshitted.

"If you see a car that's weaker than everyone else in the class, just stay away from them or tap them. The prize money isn't worth hurting somebody over."

"Go for the tires. Try to break a tie rod; broken tie rod is the best way to take a guy out. Hit him where he's weakest."

"You'll forget all of this the second that whistle blows. You'll just get heavy on the gas and try to hit something."

"If you hit a driver's side door the best thing to do is just apologize. It happens and ninety percent of the drivers understand it."

"If you see smoke coming out of a car that means their radiator is going. Hit them square on and punish that radiator."

"Some guys bust the top strap of their seat belt off and just run the lap belt?"

"Why?"

"They're dumb. Why would anyone do any of this?"

"Everyone does something stupid. One year we prepped a car, put Sean in it, and it died after one hit. We forget to add gas."

"I've been to derbies and seen cars have the airbags go off."

We talked and worked all day. Working some of the time, talking all the time.

"Brian was the best man at my wedding, but he was holding my kid so Adam held the rings. Right when the pastor needed them Adam fumbled and dropped them in the tall grass. There we were, all three of our big asses sticking out as we crawled around looking for the rings."

"I think you should have to get drug tested if you're on welfare." Brian said later that afternoon. "Why not? People say, 'well other government workers get paid by tax dollars and they don't get tested'. Well you know what? Test me. I've never done a drug in my life and I don't drink, so test me. And I'll tell you something else, I know guys who smoke pot before work then just sit there and zone out for hours. They're getting a paycheck, that's stealing, that's stealing exactly like the fake welfare recipients. There's no difference. If you draw money from the government then you ought to be tested, from welfare all the way through the president."

Soon it was time for my first test drive. I crawled through the passenger side window and fired it up. Damn it was loud! I threw it into gear and hit the gas. It really did feel like something out of a Mad Max movie. I ripped around Brian's three acres, flooring it and doing a few donuts.

"How's it feel?"

"I dig it."

"Come on, let's head into town. We need to get a new radiator hose, this one's leaking."

Brian and I hopped into his truck as Sean and Adam settled into lawn chairs next to Brittney, Ashley, and the kids.

"Where did you meet your wife?" I asked as we drove into town.

"We worked together at KFC, that's a chicken place, Kentucky Fried Chicken."

"Yeah, we have it in Michigan."

"I was 18, she was 16. She called me and asked me to the dirt races."

"The what?"

"Small oval track races on dirt. So we started dating, she was only my third girlfriend ever. Sean met Ashley in High School too, that's pretty normal around here."

"How long have you been married?"

"Two years. But we started living together in 2009. Actually, I started living with her over at her parent's place. 2009 was a rough year for me."

"Why? If you don't mind."

"I don't mind. Well first my aunt died. Then my grandma died. So my dad lost both his sister and his mother at the same time. Then my mother got a brain tumor. My mom was sick all the time; she couldn't work, and my dad took a lot of time off to take care of her. He took so much time that he basically couldn't work either, so the Sheriff came one day and told us that the house was in foreclosure and we had thirty days to get out. So, I moved in with Brittney's parents."

"Is your mom still alive?"

"She is."

"Glad to hear that."

"My dad was always good to me when I was growing up, he supported me and all, but he never really told me that he loved me, or that he was impressed by me, or proud of me. I think that's why I'm too nice to people now, I want people to like me. I think I'm trying to make the world love me, and I do derby to impress people.

Last year I bought sixteen hundred dollars' worth of steel. Well guys kept coming over 'cause they needed a bar for their car, or even a full cage, or whatever, next thing you know more than half of it was gone and I hadn't even used any of it in my own cars. My wife's putting a stop to that though.

I might have some aggression too. Some meat heads go to the gym and lift, I like to crash cars."

We pulled into AutoZone and waited in line for about fifteen minutes. When it was our turn Brian told them the type of hose that he needed and the guy went into the back to look for it. Brian and I wandered around the store waiting for him to come back. He stopped at the battery section, starring at a battery like Dipstick looked at the girls at The Fox Hole.

"What are you looking at?"

"The D34-78 Optima Deep Cycle and Starting Battery. It can stand up to any abuse, provides two times the power, spill proof, recharges faster, holds up under extreme vibration. If this battery can't start your car, nothing can. Sean and I have wanted one for a long time." It had a list price of $264.99. Brian looked at it like Ralphie looked at the Red Rider BB gun.

When the man came back he told us that they didn't have the hose in the store, they would have to order it. Brian said no thank you and we left.

"There's an O'Rielly's close to here, we'll grab the hose there." We drove over to O'Rielly's and waited in line there. After about half an hour it turned out that they also did not have the hose we needed.

We climbed back into Brian's truck to continue chasing that goose. "You want some lunch?", he asked.

"Sure."

We sat at the counter of Allison's Finer Diner. The old people all talked to each other and knew the waitresses by name. I had a grilled chicken breast, rice, and snap peas. It was all surprisingly good.

"Were you always into derby?"

"No. I used to ride four wheelers with a group of guys, but they just stopped every two miles to drink a beer and I'm not into that. Adam and Sean don't really drink much either, they're just good guys."

"Was your dad in derby?"

"No, he thinks it's a waste of time and money. And I guess he's right, but you have to have some fun in life too."

After lunch we went to Advance Auto Parts. We waited there for about another twenty minutes until we were told that they also did not have the hose we needed. After looking for a simple hose for close to half the day now, and striking out at three stores, we had no choice but to order it. They said it would arrive around

10 am tomorrow.

We drove back to the house, about three hours later, still without a new hose.

When we pulled back into the house Adam was holding something in his left hand. "Hey Brian, we found one of them hoses in the back of your garage."

Later that afternoon I went for my second test drive. This time I put all of my safety gear on. Before leaving Michigan, I had stopped by my friend Ele Bardha's house and borrowed a fire suit from him.

Ele was a stuntman. He's done three hundred commercials and over eighty-five films, including "Transformers: The Last Knight," "Baby Driver," "Batman v. Superman: Dawn of Justice," "Deadpool" and others. "I'm scared of half of the things I get involved with, but there's no quitting. That attitude doesn't comply with my line of work. The things most people are scared of are the things I tend to steer myself toward."

As I tried on a small rib protector that he handed me, I couldn't help but understand.

He also loaned me fire proof socks, gloves, face mask, and a small chest protector. In addition to all of that I had two neck braces, elbow pads, knee pads, and my helmet.

Now, over at Brian's house, I pulled all that stuff on. I was hot as Hades and stiff as a board. I drove forward just fine, but I couldn't turn my head to see to either side, and turning around to see in reverse was out of the question.

"How was the car?"

"Ran fine, but I'm going to have to cut back on some of this gear."

"Kind of figured you would, but I wanted to leave it up to you. And remember, if at any point you don't feel safe, or just don't want to go through with it just say so. We won't think anything less of you." He was trying to be nice, but it was the only thing he said to me all weekend that pissed me off.

"Don't worry about me, I'm driving."

Brittney and Ashley made chicken, green beans, and mashed potatoes for dinner. It was Sean's birthday and they baked him a cake with a demolition derby car on it. He turned 26 by the way, not 46.

We turned on the TV while we ate. The Rocky marathon was on. We watched the end of Rocky and the first parts of Rocky 2.

"You want to paint that car?"

"Let's do it."

I had picked out royal blue with white trim. The four of us painted with rollers and brushes. It actually came out a lot nicer than I thought it would.

"Have you picked out a number?" Adam asked me. "I always run number 9."

"Any reason?"

"I was born on September 9th, so that's nine-nine. I figure nine must be lucky for me."

"Why don't you run ninety-nine?"

Adam sat there for a moment. "I don't know. I just run nine."

"Should we put Obama on the side?" Sean joked. "Get him beat up in the pits."

"How about we write Hilary on the car and give it the number 2016?"

"Naw, getting him beat up is funny, Hilary would get him shot."

"I'm going with yankee927."

We painted it up. When we were done, we stood around admiring it. It was beautiful, almost too nice to crash.

On Memorial Day morning we drove to the fairgrounds.

Memorial Day is an American holiday, observed on the last Monday of May, honoring the men and women who died while serving in the U.S. military.

Originally known as Decoration Day, it originated in the

years following the Civil War. "Designated for the purpose of strewing with flowers, or otherwise decorating the graves of comrades who died in defense of their country during the late rebellion, and whose bodies now lie in almost every city, village and hamlet churchyard in the land," General John A. Logan proclaimed.

During World War I the United States found itself embroiled in another major conflict, and the holiday of Decoration Day evolved into Memorial Day, commemorating American military personnel who died in all wars, including World War II, The Vietnam War, The Korean War and the wars in Iraq and Afghanistan.

For decades, Memorial Day continued to be observed on May 30, the date Logan had selected for the first Decoration Day. But in 1968 Congress passed the Uniform Monday Holiday Act, which established Memorial Day as the last Monday in May in order to create a three-day weekend for federal employees; the change went into effect in 1971. The same law also declared Memorial Day a federal holiday.

It will forever be unclear when and where the first Decoration/Memorial Day was held, but here is a nice story, as accurate as any other: Records show that one of the earliest Memorial Day commemorations was organized by a group of freed slaves in Charleston, South Carolina less than a month after the Confederacy surrendered in 1865.

I am going to recognize that as our country's first Memorial Day. I cannot prove it, but nor can I find a historian to contradict it.

Brian drove his truck, hauling the yankee927 car while I followed behind with Adam in the passenger seat.

We passed a billboard with a picture of John Wayne. It read "I don't much care for quitters son." I took it as a sign; there was no way I was backing out.

We pulled into the Morrow County fairgrounds and headed to registration.

"I'm sorry about all the paperwork hun, you know how lawyers is." A large lady handed me one page of paper, half of it empty.

"No problem." I filled it out and handed it back to her.

"You got insurance?" She asked with a heavy emphasize on the in.

"Yes."

"Ok." She checked a box.

"Would you like to see it?"

"No."

"Ok."

"You got a valid driver's license?"

"Yes."

"Ok." She checked a box.

"Would you like to see it?"

"No."

"Ok."

"You're in, good luck hun."

Brian and I walked the fairgrounds. I told him that I would not search for the biggest hillbilly and write a slam piece about them, but I had also told him that I was going to tell the truth. Brian, Adam, and Sean were a cut above the rest. They just happened to live here and they just happened to like crashing cars. There were others there like them. We met a few guys who seemed pretty normal, just nice guys with an abnormal hobby. Having said that, overall, it was everything that you'd expect it to be. Terrible tattoos, missing teeth, camouflage clothing for no reason, fat children, and zero, and I do mean zero, minorities. The entire place was one big rebel flag fest. Half of the cars had the Rebel flag painted on their roof, their helmets, or just a full Rebel flag flying off the back of the car.

I've always hated that ridiculous Rebel flag. It's fine as a part of our history, and ignorant people have a perfect right to their freedom of speech and to fly it privately, but didn't these people realize that Ohio is north of the Mason Dixon line? If the Civil War was going on today then number one, they would be fighting for the North, and number two, they would be taking their orders from me.

Morrow County did its part for the North during the Civil War furnishing Company I, Third Regiment, Ohio Volunteer Infantry and Company G, Twentieth Regiment.

According to the book History of Morrow County, Ohio, by Abraham J Baughman, "The men of the North who enlisted at that call were regarded by all classes of society as heroes. The wearing of the army uniform was the highest distinction a man could have at that time... It is proper to say that a few fathers and mothers gave half a dozen sons, and others gave all that they had. Many of them paid the last full measure of devotion to their country with their lives upon the battlefield, and others came home bearing scars from honorable wounds and maimed for life."

I wondered; how would these men would feel about their grandchildren's grandchildren flying that ridiculous Rebel flag?

"So," I asked Brian, "you think having Yankee painted on the side of my car is going to make me a target?" I grinned.

"Joel, half of these guys don't even know what a Yankee is."

I stopped. "No. How is that possible?"

"Look at them. I don't think they all know what the Rebel flag is. You know since you've been here it's really opened up my eyes. All those stereotypes I didn't want you to write about, they're all true, aren't they?"

I didn't say anything.

"Let me ask you something?" He went on. "yankee927, did you really name it after your dog and the address of the house where you grew up? Or was it meant to poke the bear? You figured there would be a bunch of hicks here and you wanted to pick a fight."

"Both."

"Kind of a double entendre."

"Brian, you realize you're the only other person in the entire fairground that knows what a double entendre is."

He looked around. "Probably."

"It doesn't make any of them bad people. I'm a product of

my environment just like they are. I call myself educated because I can read, write, and speak at a level that they cannot, but in reality, I'm not any more educated than they are. They can fix cars, drive trucks, make food grow from the earth, and build homes. That's an education too, and I don't have any of it. My education doesn't make me better than any of them."

"No, and there are some great gentlemen in this sport. I really love my friends, the building of the cars, the events, and some of the guys I see here, but there are a lot of, well, you can see for yourself... Sean and I have already been talking about doing something else. The last three of these we've gone to have had fist fights. It's not any fun to throw yourself in front of a mob so they don't run over your wife and your kid."

So who were these demolition derby drivers and fans? And why were they here? They don't do it for the money, most demolition derby drivers will tell you. It's about the family, the memories, the rush.

"I bought this thing on Monday for $300," said 15-year demo driver Nathaniel Bray, as he unloaded his black and pink, stripped down car from his trailer.

"PPK, that's me," said Greg Kight, of the initials spray painted on his car. Kight started in derbies at age 12. "Papa Kight, PPK, that's what my grandkids call me. They're all up in the stands watching."

Kight's son, Kyle, and son-in-law, Jeff Hoitt, were there to lend a hand. All three would drive on the following night.

It can be a dangerous sport, demolition derby. Kyle, who makes vehicle windows by day, was missing nine teeth due to having a car dropped on his face. He and a friend were working on a car when a jack slipped, leaving him pinned. The friend left.

"Someone called 911, but the only person who showed up was a cop. They thought I was going to be DOA. I went to the hospital, got out and went back and kept working on the car."

Drivers are no strangers to pain. "I've been sore for a couple weeks after these things," said Greg. "If you don't see a hit coming you can get whiplash pretty bad."

Brothers Anthony and Benjie Meulen, Kyle's cousins, parked their trucks and trailers a few spots down.

This would be Anthony's fifth time participating in a derby, Benjie's been wrecking for 20 years.

"It's a big rush and that rush is super addicting," said Benjie, as he unloaded his bright orange car with the word 'Hillbilly' on the side. "It's about the fun."

About half the people at the fairgrounds ate a fried pork tenderloin before the derby got underway.

Three high school girls in bikinis, high heels, and Derby Queen sashes walked by us.

The guys and I backed yankee927 off of the trailer and gave it one last inspection before lining it up with the other 80s stock class cars.

I had a look at this hunk of Mad Max metal and couldn't help but think of its history. This was a 1983 Cadillac, a luxury car, a status symbol. At one point in its life a man brought it home, brand new, and proudly parked it in front of his home. It could have belonged to either one of my grandfathers. I'm sure the man pulled it out every weekend to hand wash it, tried not to park too close to others in the office lot for fear of getting a scratch on his door, probably drove around the neighborhood, window down, cigarette hanging from his mouth, letting everyone see him in his new Cadillac. Now it would be my weapon of destruction.

"Hey Joel." Brian called to me. "I got someone I want you to meet."

He introduced me to his friend Tim Jensen and to Tim's father Rick. "Tim started running derby when he was twelve years old", Rick told me. "I'd sign up under my name, then I'd let him drive. He probably run two thousand of them."

"Wow."

"He won two hundred or so now, maybe three hundred. He wins just about every time now, at least in the top three. He'll win today, you'll see. He could drive the worst car out here and still win. I taught him to drive derby myself. You could fill the fairgrounds with the trophies he's won. He'll win today, you'll see."

"So Tim, what do you want the world to know about you?"

"Nothing. I'm just a quiet guy. Have fun out there."

"You want to take a look at the other cars?" Brian asked me.

"Yeah."

Sixty or so cars were lined up into four classes: compact, midsized, 80s stock, and modified. The cars were brightly spray painted with numbers, initials, and monster teeth.

"I like the 80s stock class the best myself." Brian told me. "You've got more metal around you. The compact class is crazy."

"They're all crazy Brian."

"Well crazier then. The cars are tiny, but they can get up to speed fast and hit hard."

We checked out the rest of the 80s stock cars that I would be butting heads with. Some of them were banged to hell, others didn't have a scratch on them. Some seemed a lot more reinforced than mine, but others were quite a bit less. I was driving a car that was solidly in the middle of the pack.

One thing that seriously surprised me though, nobody paid as much attention to protecting the driver's side door as I did! I was the only car who had filled the driver's door with cement, I was the only one with an external bar welded across the door, and I was the only one with a cage built over the window.

My eyes drifted over to the fourth row of cars, the modified class. "Man, these things are beasts."

"Yeah, they're tanks. They allow a lot more in the modified class."

"Some of these cars look like they have some money put into them too."

"Ten to twenty k would be normal for this class. Not including all the hours in labor."

"Holy shit! Twenty thousand dollars???"

"Yeah, some of them could be over that."

"Twenty grand? To crack up a car? What... But... How?"

"I don't know."

"Brian, I've been wandering around all day. I don't see any-one here who looks like they have twenty grand to throw away."

"Oh, they don't."

"Then how…"

"For some of them, derby comes first. They can't pay their mortgage and the sheriff comes to take their home away, that's ok by them so long as they can keep their derby car. They can always live in their cousin's tool shed."

"I have no idea what to say about that."

"Like I said, we're not all like that. I only spend my overtime money, and only part of that. I put a grand into a car and I can run it three or four times. That's my season. Same with Sean and Adam, and there are a lot of other smart gentlemen out here too. But I have to admit, you've opened my eyes to the fact that there are a lot of Doofuses and Dipsticks in this sport."

"Speaking of which, where are those two clowns?" Sean, Ashley, Brittney, and Adam, were all sitting by Brian's truck. They had set up a canopy, brought lawn chairs, sodas, and waters, and settled in for the day. I hadn't seen Doofus and Dipstick since I'd arrived.

"I didn't want to point them out but…"

Five cars behind me was an old 80s Buick that they had thrown together at the last minute. The doors were held shut by coat hangers, scraps of glass were still in the windows, the Rebel flag was painted all over the sides. They were arguing about who would get to drive, both were already about half a dozen beers deep.

"It's easy to break up with a girl." Brian looked at them. "I don't know how to break up with guys. I just wish they would stay in the holler."

"In the what?"

"Oh, sorry, local expression. The holler, around here it means like the deep woods, or the outback in Australia, or some-thing like that."

"Ah. Ohio is so close to Michigan that I haven't noticed

many different expressions yet, that's interesting. You know what I have noticed?"

"What's that?"

"Other than you, nobody uses the words 'to be'."

"To be?"

"Yeah, guys will say 'The muffler needs changed' instead of saying 'The muffler needs to be changed'. Or, 'the grill needs cleaned', instead of 'the grill needs to be cleaned.'"

"Yeah everyone around here does that. Hey race meeting is starting. Here's what they're going to tell us: don't hit the driver's side door. Then they'll go on for another ten minutes about stuff that will have nothing to do with us at all."

At the meeting they told me not to hit the driver's side door, then they went on for ten more minutes about stuff that had nothing to do with me at all.

"Come on." I said to Brian, "I want to show you something."

We stood by the trunk of my car. I turned the key and popped it open.

"Are you serious?" Brian looked at me, then he looked back at the D34-78 Optima Deep Cycle and Starting Battery.

"Well I snuck into town to buy it, hid it in my trunk, then brought you here to give it to you, so yes, I'm serious."

"Thank you man, wow." Brian threw one arm around my shoulders. "Hey Brittney! Guess what Joel did?"

"Brian's not used to getting anything." Sean stuck out his hand for me to shake it. "People just take and take and take from him."

The compact cars hit the arena.

Rain drizzled as the sun peeked through the overcast skies, creating beautiful lighting over the derby's muddy stage. Hundreds of fans helped the announcer count down the start.

The twenty compact cars went full throttle, banging and bashing their cars against one another. Smoke billowed, drivers yelled, fires flared and mud flew. There was even a rainbow.

The midsized would be next, then I'd be up in the 80s stock

full sized class. I threw my fire suit on. Of the eighty or so total cars running today, exactly one driver wore a fire suit, me. Under the suit I put a small, tight fitting, rib protector on. Some of the other drivers laughed at me a little bit. Let them.

"Hey. What ya got there? Protection? Hep, hep, hep, hep, hep…"

"You know you're gonna be too hot in that!" Another driver said to me. He was wearing shorts and a T shirt. He was right, I was way too hot already. Who cares? If there happened to be a fire, I'd get out alive and most likely without any burns at all.

"I wear a fire suit every time I drive." Brian told me. "It's just smart."

"Don't worry; it's not getting to me."

"So you're going to go through with it?"

"With what?"

"Driving."

"Of course. Come on man."

In the background I heard the loudspeaker. "That's it folks, the compact class is over. Tim Jensen is your winner!"

A few minutes later the midsized cars entered the arena.

"Have fun." Brian told me. I put on the rest of my gear, climbed through the passenger side window, and fired yankee927 up. The race officials led us up to the track and got us ready to enter as soon as the midsized class was done.

I couldn't see the track, but I was close enough to hear it all now. As I sat in my car, sweating, I felt like Russel Crowe in Gladiator, waiting for his turn to enter the arena.

Engines fired all around me. The noise of medal on medal crashes cracked in the arena, followed by the roar of the crowd. Two thousand people filled the stands now, crazed for carnage.

Twice the event was stopped due to fires in the cars. Let them laugh I said again; I'll wear my fire suit gladly.

I closed my eyes and kept myself calm. In my head I heard Mickey's voice. "Stand up God Damn ya! Listen to me Rocky, you got to fight him hard!" All I had to do was push my gas pedal all the way down and fight hard. If I did that, then I would be alright, and

I would do that.

There was one final crash, one final roar from the crowd, and the midsized event was over.

"That's it ladies and gentleman." The loud speaker crackled. "And your winner, two classes in a row, Tim Jensen."

Tim drove by me, holding a checkered flag and waving to the crowd. A few other cars limped out on their own, the rest were nothing but dead bodies, dragged out of the arena by a tractor.

"And now it's time for the 80s full sized stock class!" I fired the engine up and put my visor down.

An official led us into the arena. I was instructed to pull in, head first, against one of the walls. Ten of us would start on one end, ten on the other. When the buzzer sounded we would all back into each other and then it would be every man for himself.

Twenty cars, all with v8 engines, no mufflers, RPMs through the roof, and thousands of fans screaming at the same time. I heard nothing, but everyone could feel the excitement.

I looked up to see an official counting down, already at five. This was it! Four! Three! Two! One! I threw the car into reverse and slammed the gas! A moment later I crashed, rear end to rear end with another monster. I didn't even feel the impact.

I threw it into drive, a few small shots defected off me, I looked for a target. There it was, twenty feet in front of me, a brand new bright red car without a mark on it. The passenger side was facing me, it was perfect. I slammed the gas and aimed for the passenger side front tire.

Boom! My first hard hit! I slammed into the red car, crunching in the front panel.

I threw yankee927 in reverse and navigated backwards till I lightly hit another car, then I threw it into drive and went at the red car again. Boom! This time I targeted the rear tires. I hit him hard, ending his night.

I threw it in reverse again and looked for another target. Now I was stuck. Four or five of us were grouped together, all fighting to get free. I swayed back and forth, pushing and getting pushed.

Space appeared. I found a target. I slammed the gas. Nothing happened. My engine was dead. No! No! I don't want to be out! I tried to fire it up. Black smoke poured out of the exhaust pipes that stuck up through the hood. The car rumbled but didn't turn over. Come on! Then it roared back to life! I pumped my right hand in excitement and slammed the gas. The noise was beautiful!

Half the cars were out now, lying dead along the walls. All the way across the track I spotted a big station wagon pushing another guy up against the wall. I had a clear shot all the way. I slammed the gas and went at him full throttle. I fired yankee927 across the track, gaining speed, never taking my foot off the floor.

Bang! I crashed right into his rear end, crumbling it up, breaking his rear axle, and ending his night. My second kill!

I put the car in reverse, but it would not go. I tried again. I put it into drive and slammed the gas, then tried reverse again.

The car jolted forward. My helmet cracked off the side window cage. I had just taken a massive hit in the passenger side rear fender.

I turned around to look at the guy who hit me and I gave him a big thumbs up.

Black smoke poured out of my exhaust. I tried reverse again, slammed the gas, still nothing.

A race official caught my attention, looked at me, and told me to shut it down.

"You did great man. Seriously, you drove like someone with a few events under your belt."

"Thanks for this Brian, for all of it."

As I drove away from the fairgrounds that evening, I had to tap my brakes in order to avoid hitting a Toyota that turned into my lane. Every instinct in me screamed to slam the gas! Hit him hard! Take his tires out!

I eased my car past him and continued on my journey home.

GARY LEFFEW'S BULL RIDING SCHOOL

"Today I was going to ride a bull. I hadn't stretched, I hadn't slept, and I don't know a damn thing about bull riding."

Eight seconds doesn't really sound like a long time. Well, if you find yourself clinging to the back of a gigantic, angry bull, then it suddenly feels a lot longer.

A decade ago, in college, my buddy Nate Spencer and I got it into our heads that we would be bull riders. I have no idea where this idea came from. I really don't know if it was his or mine, and I have even less of a clue as to why either one of us would have it in the first place. We were both city boys, college boys, fairly normal guys no matter how "awesome" we liked to think that we were. Neither of us grew up on a farm, knew any bull riders, or even watched bull riding on TV. The idea made no sense at all, but the idea was there. We would talk about going to Gary Leffew's bull riding school for an hour or so, then drop it.

The idea would lay dormant, sometimes for days, sometimes for two or three years, then, like the locusts that rise up every 19 years, it would once again be at the tip of our tongues.

Bull riding originated in charreadas, contests of ranch and horsemanship skills that developed on the haciendas of Old Mexico. First termed jaripeo, bull riding was originally a variant of bull fighting where riders would literally ride the bull to death. It later evolved into an event where participants merely rode the bull until it tired and stopped bucking.

By the mid-1800s, charreada-style competition became popular in the Southwest, particularly in Texas and California where Mexican and Anglo ranch hands worked together. In 1852, the Lone Star Fair held in Corpus Christi, Texas, became the first-ever Anglo-American organized event to host charreada-style bull fighting.

Jaripeo, bull riding, was featured as a secondary event, but was so popular that it made newspaper headlines as far away as New Orleans. During this time, Wild West shows also began adding bull riding to their acts.

Bull riders broke away from the traditional rodeo scene and created their own organization and governing rules in 1992. Believing that bull riding, the most popular rodeo event, could stand alone without sharing the limelight, 20 bull riders—including Ty Murray, Tuff Hedeman, and Cody Lambert—gathered in a hotel room in Scottsdale, Ariz., and each contributed $1,000 to the creation of the Professional Bull Riders, Inc, the PBR.

The PBR now hosts more than 300 events across the nation, and their World Finals in Las Vegas brings in more than 70,000 fans to catch the action. Today, bull riding is considered the fastest growing sport in the United States.

Nate and I, suburban college boys, were obviously PBR material. We owned cowboy boots and everything.

College came and went, as did the few years after it when we lived together, working and partying on the outskirts of our old campus. In time we got girlfriends, jobs, Nate got married. Talk of Gary Leffew and his bull riding school became less and less until, ultimately, it disappeared forever.

In the back of our minds, I think we both always knew that it wasn't something we were going to do. The thing was, I was about to do it. It was a beautiful summer's eve, I had the top down, duffle bag in the back, and I was driving north to the Muxlow farm for three days of instruction from rodeo legend Gary Leffew.

The Muxlow Ranch was located in Brown City, Michigan.

When I go somewhere, I like to write a paragraph or two

about that town. I try my best to find something interesting to bring you – maybe they're famous for making the world's supply of toothpicks, perhaps it is the birthplace of the waterslide, or the home of the guy who broke a German code and helped us win WW2.

I tried to find you something interesting about Brown City. There's nothing interesting about Brown City.

It's been around since 1879. It used to be a railroad stop. Now it is not. They have a lot of lumber and grain. There just isn't a whole lot for me to go on.

Apparently, the citizens felt the same way. I can just picture the first town meeting.

"Ok folks, first order of business is the name. Now Frank has suggested Brown City. I'm going to be honest with you all, that's, well, that's just not very good."

"Have you seen this place Earl? It is brown."

"Well, yeah, yeah I have. But still I don't love the name. I just don't think we're going to bring in tourists with a name like Brown."

"Just put it to a darned vote."

"Ok, ok… All in favor of Brown City?" Earl would then look around the small church with eight not so concerned citizens sitting in it. A man is reading a newspaper, a woman is knitting. Frank, an old farmer who's excited to get to name a city, raises his hand.

"Ok, that's one vote for Brown. Just Frank." Frank lowers his hand. The man next to him flips his newspaper.

"And all those opposed?" Nobody moves. "Really people? Nobody cares? Ok, fine. From this day forward we shall be known as Brown City."

A hundred and forty years later, I arrived in town.

Around ten pm I rolled my 1966, fire engine red, Ford Mustang convertible up the driveway of the Muxlow family farm. The first guys I met were brothers Tim and Nate Muxlow and their best friend, Scrubs. The farm had been in the Muxlow family for generations, their parents lived next door, their deceased grandfather haunted the old farmhouse.

"This place is seriously haunted." Nate told me. "Lights turn on all by themselves. One time I turn all the lights out, come back into the room a few minutes later, they're all on again."

"One time my VCR was turned off with the power off too, and the tape just ejected." Tim told me.

"VCR?" I laughed. "Get Netflix, your grandfather won't know how to use it."

"I felt a man's arm brushing all up against me." Tim's girl-friend said.

"Yep, that sounds like grandpa alright!" Nate laughed.

"Another time," she went on, "I come into the kitchen and the timer set itself for thirty minutes. Nobody set it, it just start ticking down on its own."

"I'd take that to mean that I have thirty minutes to pack my shit and get the hell out of Dodge." I told them.

"I never thought about it like that!" Scrubs laughed. "So, where you want to sleep?"

After setting up my air bed I wandered out to the campfire to meet some of the other guys. They slouched around in lawn chairs, looking down at their feet or stared straight into the fire. The first thing that struck me about them was how little they were.

Every sport has a body type that works best for that sport. Distance runners are skinny, swimmers are long with lean muscle, gymnasts are short and incredibly built. I had assumed that bull riders would all be huge. I just figured that you would need long legs to wrap around the bull and an amazing amount of muscle to hold yourself in place. I'm 5'10 and 175 lbs, I thought I'd be the smallest guy here. I pictured them all being 6'4 and over two hundred pounds. In reality the average size was about 5'7 and a hundred and thirty pounds.

I was also shocked at how young they were. At sixteen, Michael was already a professional bull rider. The most experienced of the group, he estimated that he had been on somewhere between twelve hundred to fifteen hundred bulls. His traveling partner, Morgan, was nineteen. Orie was fifteen but didn't look a day over thirteen.

"So how many bulls you been on Joel?" Michael asked me.

"None. Actually, I've never even seen a bull." That wasn't entirely true of course. I've driven down country roads and seen bulls standing in fields fifty yards back, I'd seen bull riding on TV, I attended a bull fight in Spain. What I really meant was, I've never been up close to a bull. Never looked a bull eye to eye and thought, "Gee, I'd like to ride that."

"Well come on then." Orie said and stood up. "Let's show you some bulls."

The next thing I knew I was following a fifteen-year-old boy and his friends into a bull pen. I wasn't leaning against the outside of the solid metal fence and looking at bulls, like a sane person, I was climbing over the fence and into an arena that was full of bulls. It was like going into the demolition derby arena, on foot.

I was hardly the first fool to test fate around bulls. There are cave drawing of young men taunting bulls.

Bull-leaping originated in Ancient Greece. It is a form of non-violent bull fighting involving an acrobat leaping over the back of a charging bull. The sport survives in modern France, Spain, and India.

Bull-fighting is still a wildly popular sport in Spain and all-over Latin America. The bulls are bred for aggression, I imagine that the matadors are too. The contest ends when the matador has used his sword to kill the bull. Normally. Every once and a while, the bull wins.

Bull-baiting was an English, and greater United Kingdom, sport. It pitted a bull against a number of dogs which were bread and trained to fight, and kill, bulls. These dogs were known as bulldogs.

The English watched their bull-baiting from a safe distance, letting the dogs do the real work. They may have been cruel, forcing one animal to fight against another, but at least they weren't fools.

Or are they? Every year the inhabitants of the small rainy island head South to Spain to join in on the annual Running of the Bulls. Bulls are released into the street, people run. That's more or less the gist of it. The English who visited to run with the bulls were fools. So was I.

"This doesn't seem that smart," I said aloud as I stood in the middle of the bull ring.

"It's fine." Orie told me.

I thought of some of the things that my buddy Metzler and I thought were fine back when we were fifteen. Jumping onto and off of moving trains, hanging our heads out of sunroofs and shooting bottle rockets at other cars, jumping off roofs and into swimming pools. There is a reason why the army has a guy in his 30s leading a bunch of kids in their late teens; somebody has to have the common sense to realize that a situation is not fine. Standing in an arena full of bulls was not fine. Yet here I was.

"So, what kinds of injuries have you guys seen?"

"Nothing big. Broken legs, broken arms, guys getting kicked in the head. Normal stuff."

"I seen a guy get his nuts stomped on."

"I seen a guy lose an eye."

"This one guy had to get thirty-seven stitches in his nut sack. One of his nuts was dangling all loose"

"That's not true, I know that guy. It was only fifteen stitches."

I stayed up and talked to the guys till about two am.

The Muxlow brothers had found me a woodshed with a small bed in it. I sat there, at two am, thinking "What the hell am I doing?" Tomorrow I was supposed to ride a bull. But why? Why would anyone in his right mind ever, under any circumstances, want to ride a bull? I didn't want to lose an eye. I didn't want do get my head kicked in. I certainly do not want to see one of my nuts hanging loose as we drive to the hospital to get fifteen to thirty-seven stitches put into my sack. In short, I didn't want to ride a bull.

It had all sounded so good on paper. Hemingway wrote about it. Incredibly brave cowboys did it. It was a man's sport. But riding a bull is not brave, it is stupid.

Bravery is understanding that you are putting yourself into harm's way, yet doing it anyway, because you have to, not because you want to. Rescue a child from a fire and you are brave. Set a house on fire then see if you are able to run from room to room without getting hurt and you are an idiot.

I did not need to ride a bull. I lay there, in the dark, wishing it was Nate Spencer who was about to ride a bull and not me! I honestly thought about packing up my stuff, I didn't have much, and getting back into my car. But what kind of a book would that be? I would have to come up with a new title. A Coward, A Mustang, and The United States of America. It didn't have the same ring to it. No, I would stay. Tomorrow I would ride a bull and for years to come I would be able to say that I did it.

Yet I did not sleep. I could not sleep. I lay awake until close to four in the morning. Finally, overcome with weariness, I fell into a deep sleep.

"Bzzzzzz" My hand swatted around my ear. Half awake I rolled over and pretended I didn't hear it.

"Bzzzzzz" I tried to ignore it. If it were a fly I could have slept. If there was a guy blowing an air horn outside, I could have slept. If there was a Doberman Pincher barking his head off inside of my room, I could have slept. But I will not share my room with a mosquito. I jumped up and turned on the lights! I searched around the shed. There was no buzzing. Nothing was flying.

I looked at my phone, it was five o'clock in the morning. I had slept a grand total of one hour so far. I sat there, lights on, with my head in my hands. I needed to kill this thing and go back to bed, but you can't kill what you can't catch. I stayed silent for a long time. So did the mosquito.

Maybe I dreamt it? I knew that I had not, but it was five thirty in the morning now and my brain wasn't working correctly. I wanted an excuse to go back to bed. I flicked off the lights and hit the pillow.

"Bzzzzzz" Less than five minutes later the mosquito hovered over my face. I jumped up and threw on the lights! In a few hours I would have to deal with a full-grown bull, right now I was getting whupped by an animal that weighed less than a sunflower seed.

I paced the room. Three or four times I found it, then lost it in the light. Once or twice I violently slapped my hands together only to come up empty. Then, finally, I killed it!

It was now six fifteen in the morning. A rooster yelled outside of my door. I stepped outside to take a piss, the ground was moist with dew, the sun was rising, and I was dead tired.

I turned off the lights, flopped into my bed, and instantly fell back into my deep sleep.

At seven thirty my alarm went off. I sat on the edge of the bed for all of thirty seconds. At the end of those thirty seconds the snooze on my alarm went off, indicating that I had actually been sitting there for a full ten minutes. I pulled on my boots, checked my pants for balls, and wandered out into the daylight. Today I was going to ride a bull. I hadn't stretched, I hadn't slept, and I don't know a damn thing about bull riding.

It was time for breakfast. The Muxlow women had made us a filling country breakfast; eggs, bacon, biscuits, gravy, and coffee. It would kill most of them by the time they were sixty, but it tasted good and it was exactly what I needed this morning. I filled up a plate and took a seat with the guys.

A lot of the guys wore bracelets that read "Be Caleb tough." I asked one of them what it meant.

"Have you met Caleb yet?"

"No, I don't think so."

So I met Caleb.

All of the guys were stiff. When you ride bulls you get banged up, there just ain't no two ways about it. There is a popular saying, "When you mess with the bull, you get the horns." Well for these guys it wasn't just a saying. They all messed with bulls, and from time to time they all got the horns. Most of them were ten, even fifteen, years younger than I was, but they all walked around like a bull had just stuck his horn right up their ass. Caleb was a bit stiffer than the rest.

"So what's with the bracelets?" I asked him.

"I don't know."

"Come on Caleb, show him."

Caleb shrugged. He reached down to his boot and hiked one of his pant legs up to show me a prosthetic limb.

"What happened?"

"Car accident."

"And you still ride bulls?"

"Sure."

Caleb Griffin began riding bulls when he was eleven years old. By the time he was sixteen it was consuming his summers. Like all young bull riders dreaming of making it to the big time, he knew that the only way to get good in his sport was to get on a bull every chance that he had.

They travel from county fair to county fair, these young cowboys, riding bulls, drinking with their buddies by a campfire, chasing the barrel racer girls, sleeping for an hour or two in the back of their car, then hitting the road with their traveling partner to do it all again tomorrow. After getting beat to hell for eight seconds, on a good day, they set off for the next show, often drive ten hours or more on just a few hours of sleep.

Even at their young age, that sort of a lifestyle catches up to you. It caught Caleb. One night, in between one fair or the other, Caleb slept in the passenger seat while his buddy slept in the driver's seat. Problem was, the car was going seventy-five miles per hour at the time.

They flipped. One time, three times? They don't know. The car landed on the passenger side. After he came through, Caleb's buddy crawled out of the car, then he struggled to pull Caleb out too.

A few minutes later, while sitting on the side of the road, a party bus pulled over. Out stepped a wedding party, bride, groom, best man, maid of honor, and all the others, all in dresses and tuxedos. Two of the guys were EMTs. They called the local hospital and stayed with Caleb till the ambulance arrived.

Safely loaded into the ambulance, Caleb began his long journey to the hospital. A few miles later the ambulance was T-boned at an intersection. Caleb flew out of his gurney and smashed into a wall. The paramedic riding with him was injured. The ambulance was totaled.

Sometime later a medivac chopper arrived and brought Caleb to the hospital. He lost count of how many surgeries he had over the next month. He says it's somewhere between twenty and thirty. During one of them, they took off his leg.

"One leg or two, I got a bull rope and a dream. I ain't letting go of either." Caleb never did become a world champion, but he rehabbed, recovered, and learned to ride with one leg, making many successful 8-second rides.

Now I understood what it meant to Be Caleb Tough.

Towards the end of breakfast, it was time to meet the bull riding guru himself, Mr. Gary Leffew. A member of the bull riding hall of fame, eight-time National Finals Rodeo qualifier, and the 1970 World Champion, Gary had done it all. When the producers of the movie 8 Seconds needed a coach to teach Luke Perry how to ride bulls, it was Gary Leffew they came to.

"I'll tell ya boys," Gary smiled at us, "Rodeo ain't just the drinkin', fightin', and loose women, you're going to have to learn how to ride a bull too."

For an old bull rider, Gary was around seventy, he moved pretty well. Here's a man who ate bacon for breakfast, bacon for lunch, then drank his dinner. For years he spent his days getting slammed around by the meanest bulls that the United States of America could breed, his nights fist fighting with the other cowboys, then got three hours of sleep in the back of a pickup truck before driving nine hours to some other cowlick town just to do it all over again. By all rights he should have died of old age somewhere around thirty-seven, but he was seventy years old and he looked pretty good. No walker, no hearing aids, just a plate of bacon, a cowboy hat, and a perfect smile.

"Get your skinny butts around the TV here; we're gonna start with some video."

Surprisingly Gary was more or less a full-on yogi who just happened to ride bulls.

"The first thing I want you to do is think of your favorite bull rider. Now imagine you're him. Today you're going to do what he does, you're going to move how he moves, you're going to ride like he rides. He is a winner and so are you."

I couldn't name any bull riders, not a single one, so I didn't have a favorite. I looked over at the bulls in the pen again. Two of them had their horns locked and were pushing each other around the ring. I wondered if there were any retired bull riders that I could think of. Guys who were planning on sitting around in the shade and drinking an Arnold Palmer all day, I could picture myself doing that.

"Now today you're going to ride a bunch of bulls and you're going to be great. After your best ride today, I want you to take a moment and remember exactly how you feel. Keep that feeling, go to bed with it tonight, make love to that feeling. Let your mind know that you're a champion bull rider. Your mind will work on it all night, you'll program your mind and your mind will program you, and when you wake up in the morning, you'll be a champion. Look at great photos of bull riders in perfect form and say to yourself, that's me, next thing you know your body will move like theirs.

I went six months without riding. Bucked off of everything I sat on. Then I started visualizing. I pretended I was George Paul. For eight seconds man I rode just like him, then I heard that buzzer and the crowd roaring and I was Gary Leffew again! When I started visualizing, I knew every turn the bull was going to make boy, I could just sense it before the ride even started. I went from not being able to ride an old cow to hanging on to the toughest son bucks in the NFR."

I looked around the room. A couple of the guys were tuned in; most were refilling their coffee, playing on cell phones, or sleeping in lawn chairs. It was great advice, but most of the guys were nineteen and it's tough to tell a nineteen-year-old guy anything. All they wanted to do was ride bulls.

"Let's do some drills. Rookie, you first."

I hopped up on a wooden barrel and pretended to be a cowboy for everyone's amusement.

"Up and down boy, get some daylight between the wood and your ass, drive on your rope, don't let me see you get on them pockets!"

Strangely enough, I thought to myself, these terms are starting to make sense to me. The other thought I had was this, I'm tired. I've been on a wooden barrel for all of three minutes and the tiny muscles on the insides of my legs were beginning to get worn out. I certainly wasn't going to say anything about this to anyone, but it can't be a good sign.

I always wondered what that goofy machine at the gym was for. You know, the one that only women use, their legs going in and out like a giant butterfly. Well now I know; it was for bull riding.

"Alright boy, perfect dismount. Look over your shoulder and slide off into your hand. Hit the ground and duck down, you don't want to get kicked in the head!"

I did not want to get kicked in the head. A perfect dismount meant that you came off the left and just behind the bull. Evidently many rodeo bulls have learned this. If they can't buck you off, they like to kick you the second you dismount, learning that they should aim behind them and just to their left. When you come off, you best duck. Riding a bull was on my list of adventures, getting kicked in the head by a bull was not.

Next it was time for the drop barrel. The drop barrel was basically a wooden barrel on a teeter-totter. You sat on the wood barrel while a boy on the other end lifted you up about eight feet, like a bull jumping, then dropped you down, like a bull kicking. I jumped on. I considered letting them know that I was both afraid of heights and that I easily got motion sickness, but I couldn't think of a manly way to breach the subject. I got on the barrel and grabbed the rope, up it went.

"Drive boy! Get some daylight!"

It dropped. I almost fell, face forward, into the hard-packed dirt. This went on for another five minutes; I felt like I was the new Jewish kid at some sort of a hick elementary school.

"Alright boys, let's go buck some bulls!"

"Buck some bulls???" I thought to myself. Does this man realize that I almost fell off of the training barrel??? I'm not kidding, I honestly thought that I might get bucked off the training barrel. The training barrel!

I felt like a pilot who had four hours of ground school and was being asked to fly the plane. "Don't worry son, it's not a trans Atlantic, we just need you to do a little puddle jump from Akron to Columbus. Just put her up in the air, fly twenty or thirty people around for an hour, then touch 'er down. Nothing to it."

"Rookie!" I turned and looked at Gary. Maybe he had gotten some common sense. Obviously, he was going to tell me that I need a few more days of ground work, then I could try riding a bull on Sunday. A midget bull if he could wrangle one up.

"Yes?"

"Let's get some spurs on them boots!"

"Spurs? Won't that just piss the bulls off?"

"That's the idea son."

So Gary helped me put spurs on my boots. Scrubs very nicely lent me his safety vest and helmet, both of which I took willingly as I marched towards the bull pen.

I watched two guys climb into the ring, sporting colorful sashes and wearing running shoes instead of boots. They would be our two rodeo clowns for the day.

One of them was Nick Nagy, a full-time professional bull rider and rodeo clown. He was like a god to these boys.

Rodeo clowns date to the beginnings of competitive rodeo in the early 1900s, when promoters hired cowboys to entertain the crowd between events. These individuals began wearing oversized, baggy clothing, face paint, and put on a clown show that generally had a western/cowboy theme. When bull riding competition began to use ill-tempered Brahma bulls in the 1920s, the need for a person to distract the bull from fallen riders fell to the rodeo clown.

Today the term "rodeo clown" is now seen as somewhat derogatory. They are properly referred to as bullfighters or rodeo protection athletes. The primary job of the rodeo bullfighter is to protect a fallen rider from the bull by distracting it and providing an alternative target for the bull to attack. These individuals expose themselves to great danger in order to protect the riders. To this end, they wear bright, loose-fitting clothes that are designed to tear away, with protective gear fitted underneath.

The bullfighters do often pull double duty in many smaller shows, working as clowns to entertain the crowd between events. At the larger rodeos, the job is split into two separate ones: bullfighters who protect the riders from the bull, and entertainers who provides comic humor.

Bullfighers require speed, agility, and the ability to anticipate a bull's next move. Working closely with very large, very powerful animals, bullfighters are frequently injured, sometimes seriously, sometimes fatally.

In 2003, bullfighters in the Professional Bull Riders (PBR) organization stopped wearing traditional rodeo clown make-up & outfits, and traded them for sports jerseys & shorts with corporate sponsor logos. As I'd see over the next few days, Nick Nagy was no clown.

"You ready?" Nate Muxlow called down to me.

"Yep!" I yelled back. It was time to get into a new state of mind. I was going to ride a bull. "Let's go! Am I up first?"

"Second."

I watched Michael, the most experienced of the boys, climb onto a bull. He nodded his head and Caleb pulled open the chute. Michael's bull broke out, it reared, kicked, spun, but Michael sat on top of it like he was riding a cloud. Eight seconds later he let go, spun around and landed on his feet. The bull fighters lured the bull away from him and Michael safely climbed the fence. The guys cheered.

"You've been doing your homework son!" Gary yelled at him from the stands. "Bull riding's just like dancing with a woman boys. You ever dance with a gal who's just light as a feather in your arms? Anywhere you want her to go she's just there, you don't try to yank her around or fight with her. You let that bull lead, don't try to fight an eighteen-hundred-pound animal, just follow it around light as a feather."

I could do this. I could ride a bull. I knew that I could do this and I was ready. There are pictures of me at three years old on a horse's back, my father leading me around. By ten I was galloping with no fear. At twelve I spurred my horse forward and saved my younger sister when her horse ran away from her, earning myself a pine needle in the eye but the praise of my father in front of the entire camp. At seventeen I worked in the summer camp's barn. Later I was a full-on wrangler at the Bar Lazy J ranch in Parshall, Colorado. I may never have been on a bull before, but I understood the mechanics of how these animals moved. I was not afraid. I would absolutely stay on this bull for eight seconds.

I stepped into the chute and slid down on the bull. There was no room for my legs on either side. I was trapped in a small metal box with an enormous animal, my left wrist, my riding wrist, was still a little hurt from the demolition derby. I forgot every single thing that I had learned that morning. The guys all jabbered at me:

"Don't forget to...

"If he turns into the hand...

"Just remember...

"When you dismount...

Guys surrounded me. Six guys gave me instructions at the same time. I heard none of them. My hand was locked in so hard I thought I might lose it. My feet were down. I was as ready as I was going to get.

"Let's go." I called to Caleb, but he didn't pull the gate.

"Remember if he bucks out to get some daylight..."

"Yeah, yeah, yeah. Caleb!" I nodded at Caleb. He still didn't pull the chute. Someone was still giving me instructions, someone that outranked him and he didn't want to be rude.

"Now, when he goes into his first kick…"

"Pull the God damn chute!" I yelled at Caleb!

The chute opened and we flew out. I was riding a full-grown rodeo bull. He was a retired bull, a bit older and a bit slower than when he was throwing cowboys on the pro circuit, but he could still buck and kick. The power was unbelievable.

He may not have been in his prime, but he could still buck hard. Don't believe me? Go to a boxing gym and challenge a forty-five or fifty-year-old trainer who used to be a pro. See if he can't smash your head in.

Eight seconds sounds like a very short period of time, but time is relative. It moved slower, I could feel the bull's muscles, I could hear his breath, I felt him jump and I drove on my rope getting daylight under my ass, then pulled myself down and positioned my body for the kick. Eight seconds later I was on the ground, a decent dismount, landing on my feet and getting myself out of harm's way.

The guys cheered. It may have only been a dozen cowboys and another ten people in the stands, but it felt like a lot more to me. I had ridden a bull!

I caught my breath, grabbed my water, and sat down on the bleachers. Guys nodded at me and shook my hand.

"This game is fifty percent physical and a hundred percent mental." Gary yelled from the stands. "Ask a loser about a bull and he'll tell you 'Oh he's tough as hell, he can't be rode'. Ask a winner and he'll tell you, 'That bull ain't no big deal. Here's how you ride him'. You run with losers you're gonna become a loser. Run with winners and you'll start winning. Remember that boys. Change your friends if you have to. There ain't no spot in this game for people who drag you down."

I was glad that I rode right away. I was able to pump myself up, get up there, and do it. Now the adrenaline dumped out of my body.

I grabbed my notebook, sat back, and watched. Jessie got thrown face first into the metal fence, Chris got dumped hard the second Caleb opened the chute, fifteen-year-old Orie got bucked off then stepped on, thankfully on his safety vest. This was one rough sport. A few of the more experienced guys cycled through their second bull of the day, jumping me in the batting order, and I let them.

Tim noticed me. "You ready to ride again?"

"Hell yeah."

"I like it! Let's go."

So I pulled on my safety vest and climbed up the platform.

"Got you an intermediate bull this time. Still on the pro circuit."

"You think that's a good idea?" What I was saying, as clearly as I knew how, was "That's not's a good idea!" But the guys all thought I could do it. The next thing you know I had a circle of guys around me.

"Come on Joel!"

"Think like a winner!"

"Cowboy up!"

I decided that I did not like the term "Cowboy up". I thought to myself, maybe I'll just punch the next guy who looks at me and says "Cowboy up". How would that be? Here's a little saying I came up with: "Shut the hell up and give me a bit of breathing room. It's a huge angry bull and if I want to be scared then I'll be scared." It's not concise enough yet to be quotable or to go down as one of history's great sayings, but I'm working on it. For the time being, it gets the message across.

"How many bulls should you be on before you ride an intermediate bull?" I asked.

"Twenty-five to fifty."

"But I've been on one." I looked around to see if anyone had heard me as the circle of guys pushed me ever closer to a big black angry bull. "I've been on one." I said again, a little bit louder.

"Cowboy up!" Someone in the circle replied.

I sat down on the bull. I set my feet. I locked my hand into the rope. I nodded at Caleb.

The gate flew open. Like a comet firing towards earth I smashed face first into the arena. I hit so hard that my helmet drove itself a full three inches into the dirt, allowing the earth to come right through my mask and slap me in the face. My wrist hurt, my shoulder hurt, my face hurt, and my neck hurt. I only lay there for a second, probably much less than that, but it was enough time to have one single thought run through my mind at least a hundred times; I could have broken my neck.

People use that expression from time to time. "I slipped on the ice, I could have broken my neck." But in reality, they were nowhere near to breaking their neck. They could have broken their wrist, their tailbone, maybe cracked the back of their head, but their neck was in no real danger. Mine was. I could have broken my neck. I got thrown from a bull and landed flush on my head. It was a neck breaking injury. This may have been the stupidest thing that I had ever done.

A member of my fraternity, James Sa, ran in a race called the Warrior Dash a few years ago. He dove into a mud pit, hit the bottom, and broke his neck. Now he will be in a wheelchair for the rest of his life. I was perhaps the world's biggest idiot, and in a few hours, I was going to prove that point yet again. But first, I would eat lunch.

It's amazing how hungry I was. I inhaled food like I hadn't eaten in days. We piled our plates high with Sloppy Joe's and sat to watch some video tape of the morning's rides. I held an ice pack around my wrist, it was fractured, or at the very least sprained, and it hurt like hell if I tried to move it.

The TV was brought outside, the camera hooked up to it, and we all gathered round to watch Michael's perfect ride. I was up next.

Gary watched my first ride. "Not bad son. Driving on your rope, got some daylight between you and your pockets. Not bad at all." I felt pretty good, although I had to admit that watching it on video tape made me realize that it was not the insane bull ride that I had thought it was. Still, it was a bull, it was rearing and kicking, and I was on top of it. Not bad at all, I thought to myself as I dropped hamburger meat on the front of my shirt, picked it off with my hands, and ate it.

I ate more, spilled more, and watched the lineup of young cowboys cycle through their bulls.

Then I was in the chute again. There I was nodding at Caleb who pulled the door and out I flew. My second ride did not last as long. It didn't last at all. The only thing I can say is I really did come down as fast and as hard as I remembered, and I really did spike right onto my outstretched wrist then onto my head.

"You wanted off this bull." Gary said to me.

That comment surprised me. I really didn't know what to say. "What are you talking about?"

"Let's watch it again." Gary went back a few frames then ran it again. "Right here." He hit pause. "You're looking for a way out."

"No, I wasn't." I searched my mind. I remembered every second of the ride (both seconds of the ride to be exact). I had tried to hang on.

"Video tape don't lie son. You pussied out."

I watched the tape again. I didn't know what to say. There was nothing in me that recalled trying to get off that bull, but I watched the tape and I could see it as clearly as everyone else. It was a video of a scared man trying to get off of a bull. There were no two ways around it. My wrist felt terrible. My pride was hurt much worse.

We watched more tape. Gary lectured on breathing exercises, told us about a man named Freckles who took second place in the world at age forty-seven, about crabs pulling each other down and how important it was to surround yourself with people who would boost you up... I couldn't listen to a word of it. All I wanted to do was get on another god damn bull.

"You ready?" Tim asked me.

Lunch was done, I had requested to go first. My vest was on, my helmet was on, and my bull was loaded into the chute. I shoved my left hand into my glove and instantly I let out a grunt of pain.

"Cowboy up." Caleb said to me. I wanted to punch him, or at least tell him to shut up, but it's tough to look at a seventeen-year-old bull rider who's not complaining about the loss of a leg and whine to him that your wrist is fractured.

So instead of punching him, I nodded, and said, "Yep.", as I entered the chute.

I locked my hand into the rope, more pain. My wrist cannot handle this. It will handle this, I said to myself. It will handle this for eight seconds.

"Ok boys!"

They pulled the chute and off we went. The video tape may show that it was not the most violent bull that God ever created, but it was a bull and I rode it. I drove on my rope, I got my daylight, I stayed off of my pockets. For eight seconds the video will show that I forgot about the pain in my left hand. I cowboyed up, and for the second time that day I successfully rode a bull.

When eight seconds had passed, I dismounted. I swung my right leg over the top of the bull and leapt to the ground, just like Gary had shown us. I landed on my feet, the perfect dismount!

Then, because bulls often like to kick dismounted riders who end up behind them, I quickly dropped to my knees, driving my own spurs into my ass. A week later I'm still covered with scabs and bruises, the worst one being a black and blue mark on my ass. As long as I lived, I never assumed that I would injure myself by kicking my own ass with a pair of spurs, but that is exactly what I had managed to do.

After spending the rest of the afternoon limping around, holding my wrist, and wondering when exactly my shin started bleeding, it was time to relax. I ended up in the back of a pickup truck, a pair of barrowed shorts over my shoulder, heading to the pond.

After the day we had just had it was better than any swimming pool. We wrestled on the dock and threw each other in, jumped off a two-story platform, and propelled ourselves off the rope swing. All you could see in every direction were green fields and the setting sun. We drove back wet, drip dried, and took our places around the camp fire. Someone threw me a beer.

"It's the lifestyle." Gary said and the guys leaned in to listen to him. "Once you've lived it there ain't nothing else for ya. You work eight seconds, that's it. Then it's women and fighting. Man, we used to call it the Friday Night Fights. Every little town we went to boy, it was just a matter of time till the fight broke out. This one town, we come into the bar and start off dancin' with the girls, having some beers, you know. Little time goes by and I head out back to have a leak. Five boys followed me out and circled me up, I just about shit myself, but I was taking one of them down I promise you that.

You know, they didn't like us bull riders dancing with their women. So, they're saying this and that and starting to push me around a little bit, so I reach out to grab one of them by the neck, and I don't know what the hell I done but it just dropped him. I mean like a sack of taters, and he's gasping for air and I'm thinkin', what the hell did I just do? And them other four boys are looking at me like I'm some sort of Kung Fu master. So I yelled 'Ya'll want some of what he just got!' and they just sort of looked at each other and backed away. Man, I almost caught a beating that night."

We stayed up talking most of the night.

"I knew this Indian once named Kicking Bear." Gary started another story. "You know the Indians name their sons after the first thing they see when their son is born…"

"Yeah, I don't buy that." I told him.

"You don't?"

"Come on. How many times do you wake up in the morning, step outside your tent, and the first thing you see is a bear kicking? Never happens. If that were true there'd be a lot more Indians named Shit In The Grass."

In the typical cowboy tradition these boys wrecked their bodies in constant battles with bulls, slept little, drank before the age of twenty-one, then got up the next morning to do it all again.

It was hard to understand. But, it wasn't.

When I was younger my favorite movie was The Outsiders. In the film, based on the popular novel of the same name by S.E. Hinton, the main characters live an exciting life of never-ending youth. The gang of seven best friends included one guy with a small house on the cheap side of town. There they stayed up late, drank, laughed, fought with other groups, and bonded into a family.

Everywhere I have ever been in America, in the world, everyone wants to belong to a gang, a club, to form bonds of real friendship with people that they can count on. There really isn't that much difference between co-ops of social justice liberals and motorcycle clubs. The best moments in life are often just sitting around a fire with your pals.

The writing was on the wall for these guys. I met their fathers. Men in their 40s but already broken down from life, a dead-end job, a failed marriage, even two, and a broken body from too many bull rides.

But like the characters in The Outsiders, none of these boys would ever turn thirty. In their minds they sat around the circle of the fire in a state of perpetual youth.

I remembered sitting around with my pals at age seventeen. We ate pizza and drank milkshakes, then woke up in the morning with six pack abs. All grinning, all ridiculously handsome, all ignorant of the reality of how quickly it would be over.

But not tonight. Tonight, after three bull rides, I was accepted as a member of the gang. And I liked it.

The real cowboys weren't too much different. Cattle drives hired any man or boy who could do the work. Age, race, even your ability to speak English, none of that really mattered.

After the Civil War many former slaves went west. They were willing to work hard and take the jobs that others wouldn't. It is estimated that as many as 25%, and maybe even a third, of all cowboys were African American. Others were Mexican, Native

American, or mixed races that found it difficult to get more desirable jobs. And like the name suggests, many were boys.

In the movie The Cowboys, with John Wayne, he surrounds himself with young boys doing the jobs of fully grown men. They may have been a bit younger than average, but certainly plenty of cowboys were in their teens.

John Wayne let himself die halfway through that movie when Bruce Dern shoots him in the back. The audience couldn't believe it. Bruce Dern couldn't get another decent role for years. But The Duke understood. He knew that the young men were the real heroes of that era.

When I woke my wrist was swollen, red, and painful. It wasn't a break, but it was a bad sprain or maybe a fracture. I could cowboy up and ride with it if I wanted to, but the truth is, I didn't want to. I had done it. For one full day in my life, I was a bull rider. I was happy with that, it was enough.

I wrapped my wrist up in a tight bandage and headed out for breakfast. I grabbed some eggs and sat down at a table with Nick Nagy, professional bull fighter.

In addition to bull fighting, Nick was also a champion bull rider, amateur cage fighter, night worker at Gordon Food Service, and all-around nice guy. Every kid on the Midwestern rodeo circuit knew him, and they all loved him.

"Some of the other guys on the pro tours don't want nothing but drinking and going after girls." Nick told me. "If a kid wants an autograph or a picture then I'm going to sit there all night with them. They can talk to me all night, I don't care."

I sat with my eggs and coffee. "You mind if I follow you around today?" I asked Nick.

"Not at all. You want to do some bull fighting with me"

I thought it through, "I'll yell at the bulls from a safe distance, then jump on the fence if they look at me."

"Sounds good."

So once again I was putting on a safety vest and heading into the bull pen. I was done riding bulls, but I was hardly out of harm's way. Today I would be a bull fighter, the most dangerous job in rodeo.

When you watch a rodeo, the bulls look large. When you ride a bull, it feels like you're on top of a lightning bolt, but you don't really understand how big and scary bulls are until you're a bull fighter. Even if you're front row at the rodeo, it's just not the same as being eye level and on the dirt with them. When you go to the zoo you can stand ten feet away from a tiger without losing your breath or skipping a heartbeat. Take that fence away and the game changes.

"Alright." Nick said to me. "I want you to stand back there and stay near the fence for a while till you get used to it." He got no arguments out of me.

They let the first bull out. He kicked, spun, and bucked. It was like standing on a frozen lake while your idiot friend Metzler did donuts in an SUV. At any minute he could just run you right over and Darwin you out of existence.

The rider fell.

"Hey! Hey!" I yelled at the bull from a safe distance as Nick got the bull to chase him and the rider scrambled to safety.

On the other side of the arena Frenchy, a French Canadian whose name I never did catch, also meekly yelled "Hey!" It was his first-time bull fighting too.

A few more bulls came out and I headed for the fence as quickly as I could.

"Come on Joel!" Gary yelled from the safety of the stands. "Are you a man or a mouse?"

A couple more bulls went by and, like an idiot who thinks he knows how to ride a motorcycle so he no longer needs a helmet, I began to get more comfortable.

"Hey Frenchy!" Gary yelled as Frenchy climbed the fence to safety. "Are those your legs or are you riding a chicken?"

Another bull came out. It spun in circles five or six feet away from me, then it dumped Michael. Nick was not in position; he couldn't be everywhere at all times. I rushed in and smacked the bull on the nose as Nick dragged Michael to his feet.

The bull chased me, and boy did I run! Nick rushed back and distracted the bull, allowing me to make it to the fence.

"Good job." Nick told me.

"Thanks Joel." Michael called over his shoulder. I nodded at him. I wasn't trying to be brave, or to shut Gary and the peanut section up, I just didn't want to see a kid get hurt.

I worked the next ten or so bulls closer. Standing my ground where Nick placed me, distracting bulls when I needed to, helping riders find their way to the fence when they needed it. I have no delusions that Nick and I were doing the job 50/50, but it may have been an 80/20 partnership, maybe even 70/30 on a few of the rides. At any rate, I was doing it, I was bull fighting.

"Be careful with this next bull." Nate Muxlow called to me as he helped Jessie into the chute. "He's mean as hell."

I nodded. I would let Nick take this one. I'd wave and yell and when I was done Gary could laugh at me all he wanted to.

The bull charged out. He kicked up and dumped Jessie over his head. Ninety percent of the time riders come off to the back or the sides. Nick is at a level where he can read how the ride is going and instantly predict where and when the rider is coming off. He can do that most of the time, but of course he's not always correct.

Nick was at the most logical spot to save Jessie, which on this one rare occasion, meant he was terribly out of position. Jessie stumbled to his feet. The bull charged and scooped Jessie up by the horns, shoving him forward towards the metal fence!

I rushed in. With one hand I pushed down on the bull's nose, with the other I pushed Jessie out of the way. Then I grabbed the bull by the horns and slammed my shoulder and head into it as hard as I could. I don't know if I had any physical effect on the animal, or if the fact that a 175 lbs mammal was trying to take it head on just confused the bull so much that it stopped, but either way, I stopped it, I saved Jessie, and I made it safely to the fence.

"That was good work cowboy." Gary called to me from the stands. I'm not sure how Gary felt about me before that. He may have liked me just fine, he may not have, or he might just have seen me as another writer, but things between him and me were noticeably different after that moment.

I stayed in for a few more bulls, but twice I ran to the fence and twice my left hand failed me when I was trying to climb. It didn't cost me either time, but I was lucky. Had a bull been behind me and I slipped off the fence, well…

We broke for lunch, and I decided that I was done with bull fighting, done with bull riding, and simply back to being a writer.

"You done good." Nick told me as I sat with him and ate hamburgers and chips. "You done real good."

"I've never seen a rookie make a pass like that!" Nate told me. "Most guys just stand twenty feet back and yell, or throw their hat at the bull or something. I was like, 'Holy shit! Did he just grab a horn!' I'm serious, you could be a bull fighter, for real."

It felt good, but I didn't know what to say so I changed the subject. "The guys tell me you're a cage fighter too." I said to Nick.

"Yep, fighting tonight."

I put my hamburger down and took a few beats. "Tonight? You have a fight tonight?"

"Yeah, at seven thirty."

"And you're out here bull fighting all day?"

"Sure. What else am I going to do?"

"Rest? Relax? Warm up?"

"Nah." We're only bucking stock till three today anyway.

"Yeah, but, but, but…" But no real thought was coming out. I didn't want to say "but" twenty-eight more times, so I shoved some hamburger into my mouth. "Where do you train?"

"I don't."

"Huh?"

"I just work, you know? Bull fighting's tough work, you know that. Running sprints in the soft dirt all day. At nights I throw beef for Gordon's Food Service. I lift sixty to ninety-pound bundles of beef onto the belt. I throw between two and three thousand of them a night. When I'm not there the boss has to get two guys to cover my spot."

"So you get paid double?"

"Ha, I wish! Plus, I have to run up and down this hallway to tag them. Most guys walk the hallway, but I always run it. I figured it out once, on an average night I run seven miles in that hallway."

"And you strength train for cage fighting by throwing giant slabs of beef?"

"Yeah."

"You know you are literally Rocky Balboa."

"Ha! I never thought of it like that."

"Alright bull riders! Let's watch some video tape!" Gary shouted and we all pulled up our chairs to watch ride after ride.

The morning was brutal. Chris, a fifty-eight-year-old man who had no business bull riding, fell off his first bull the moment the chute opened. His shoulder was dislocated and he was done for the rest of camp. I'll assume for the rest of his life too. Fifteen-year-old Orie got kicked, thankfully in the training vest but it still knocked him around some. His next ride he sprained his ankle. George's leg snapped in half before he ever left the chute. The bull just slammed him so hard into the wall of the chute that the shin bone snapped right in half. It sounded like a shotgun going off. Howling in pain we tried to pull him out, but with his left hand locked in, and the bull slamming him side to side, we had no choice but to pull the gate and let him fly off of the bull's back. Right now he was on his way back to a Canadian hospital.

"Get a job you hate boys." Gary told us. "If you don't hate your job then you won't become a bull rider. But I'll tell ya, if you can do it there ain't nothing in the world like it. A different town every night, money, girls, the roar of sixty thousand people cheering for ya. Get on as many bulls as you can. You don't even start to learn till you've been on a hundred bulls."

He paused the video after Jessie's ride. He showed Jessie hung up on the bull's horns, and me rushing in to save him. He paused it when my shoulder crashed into the bull's head, bringing him to a stop, my right hand grabbing the bull's horn.

"That's working 'em close boy." Gary pointed at me and nodded. "That's how you do it."

I really hadn't realized exactly what I had done. There was no clear thought in the two seconds that it happened; I don't recall trying to be brave. But just like yesterday when Gary had paused the tape and told me that I pussied out, here was the proof that I had saved Jessie's ass. Video tape don't lie.

After lunch we went back to buck some more stock. This time I sat in the stands, left wrist bandaged up, safety vest retired and returned to Scrubs, notebook in hand. There were less riders now. I was out, Chris was out, George was gone. Some of the other guys sat with their heads in their hands and let the more experienced, braver, and more dedicated guys jump their place in line. It was only the better riders left now, and only the better bulls.

"Drive on that rope boy!" Gary yelled. Then he turned to me. It's not that he had ignored me at all for the first two days, or was in any way cold, but I felt that our relationship had changed in the instant that I pushed Jessie out of harm's way. Maybe I'm making it up, or maybe I'm not.

"Day after I get married, I come downstairs." Gary said to me. "My new wife's down there, burnt toast, eggs sticking to the pan, bacon still frozen. I said, 'What's the matter? Can't cook neither?'" Gary laughed hysterically, I chuckled politely. "Oh man, she was fit to be tied, I'll tell ya!"

"Don't get bucked off Orie!" Orie's mother called from the stands before Orie's next ride.

"Tell him to ride good." Gary said to her. "Tell him he's going to make eight seconds. When you say don't get bucked off all they hear is the negative. You got to flood his mind with positive. When I was coming up in the standings, I'd always pal around with the guy one spot ahead of me in the ranks. I'd tell him 'Don't get thrown by that turn. Don't get blasted out of the chute. Don't fall off.' Pretty soon that negative creeped in and off he goes. I always tell my students, ride well, get your winnings. Positive, positive, always positive."

In the arena, Orie got bucked off.

"I saw this gal one time at a rodeo." Gary went back to talking to me. "She was a barrel racer, you know, sixteen, seventeen years old, beautiful. I seen her and she seen me, I wasn't but nineteen years old, but I was in love. I never said a word to her, too shy back then, but she felt it too, you could just tell. So I seen her again down the road, couple rodeos later, but I don't say nothing. So I told myself, boy, next time you see this girl you're going to say something, and I watched out for her at every rodeo I went to but I didn't run into her. So then we're at some little bar somewhere, me and the guys, and I get picked up by this cougar. Thirty-five, forty years old, she takes me home and uses and abuses me…"

"You hated every minute of it I'm sure."

"Ha! Yeah so you know I get up in the morning, wander out to the kitchen to get a drink, and just then a door opens."

"Oh boy."

"Yep. There she is, the love of my live and I just spent the night with her mama. She sees me and slams the door in my face! I was in love with that girl, never did get to say a single word to her."

We broke early that afternoon and once again I found myself at the pond. This time there were a number of families there as well, so our horseplay and language calmed down a bit. In other words, I stopped pretending that I was seventeen again.

Nick spent most of the afternoon playing with three of the local kids, just judging by the way they interacted with him I assumed that they were his nephews or cousins. None of the three kids knew how to swim, so Nick treaded water while they jumped off the dock to him. He then swam them back to shore and went out for the next one.

An hour later we were again in the back of the pickup truck. Someone handed me a beer. I was pretty sure that it was illegal to drink in a car, I was also fairly sure that it's illegal to ride in the back of a pickup truck, but these were city laws and they just didn't feel like they applied out here.

"Were those your nephews?" I asked Nick.

"Who?"

"The kids you were playing with."

"Oh, no."

"How do you know them?"

"I never seen them kids before in my life. I just seen some kids that don't know how to swim so I figured I'd teach them. I just want everyone to have a good time, wherever I go I want to see people have fun. It ain't bull riding, or cage fighting, or bull fighting, it's just keeping people safe and helping someone have fun. The one thing I can't stand is seeing someone not having a good time. I'm at a bar, I'm going to get everyone dancing. I see someone in a wheelchair, I'll roll them out and dance with them. You don't have to be good, just wave your arms around and smile. We're all living, we're all breathing, I just want to see everybody happy."

"Who works your hands?" I asked Nick.

We were at an enormous steakhouse and bar in Port Huron, MI. The entire place looked like the set of Roadhouse, the Patrick Swayze movie from the 80s.

Huge bullhorns, hung above the roof of the restaurant, could be seen from the road.

The parking lot was lined with pickup trucks, Harley Davison motorcycles, and classic Detroit muscle cars. Girls walked around in cowboy boots, Daisy Duke shorts, and bikini tops. Corn fed bouncers looked over the entire scene.

It was called The Angry Bull Roadhouse. I'm not making that up.

A cage was set up in the parking lot under a street light. About five hundred people were seated around it. Ring girls in bikinis wandered around, fighters threw punches in the air. I held a pair of mitts for Nick to hit.

"What's that mean?' He slammed a few punches into the mitts. His form was terrible but he hit hard.

"Who's your boxing coach?" I knew a decent amount about

boxing. I had seventeen fights in Chicago, winning all but two of them. A few of my bouts were in the Golden Gloves. Now, from time to time, I trained boxers.

"I don't have one."

"Brazilian jujitsu coach?"

"Nope."

"Jesus man, you know you're about a go into a cage fight, right?"

"Ain't no big deal."

"Do you train at all?"

"No, don't have time. I wrestled my whole life though."

Wrestling was the best base for cage fighting. Still, I found it unbelievable that a guy with no boxing, kickboxing, or submission training was going into a cage fight.

Nick hit the mitts a few more times. Everything he did was wrong, but his raw power was unreal. I've held mitts for hundreds of guys, Nick hit extremely hard.

"Let's go." In the ring the bikini contest had just ended, it was time for Nick's bout. Along with Tim, the three of us put on cowboy hats and walked to the cage.

"Remember" I told him, "Don't fool around with him, just get a double leg takedown and pound him."

One minute and forty-seven seconds later Nick had taken his opponent down and knocked him out.

We sat around the fire that night and drank beers. The guys hovered around Nick like he was a planet with half a dozen moons.

"So I have to ask you…"

"Ask." Nick said to me.

"It just seems, well, that you're cut out for more than a night job throwing meat around."

"I want to be military."

"I think you'd be pretty great at that."

"I joined once. I was in basic and I twisted a knee. I didn't want to complain to the sergeant so I was just going to tough it out, put my pack on, just going to limp for a few days and work through it, but my sarge comes to me and asks what's wrong. So, I tell him that I hurt my knee, no big deal. So, I think they're just giving me a few days off, let me rest it and heel up. Next thing you know, I'm out. They said I'm not physically fit enough for military service."

"You're not physically fit enough for military service?" He was the most physically fit guy I knew.

"I keep sending them tapes of me bull riding, running around, cage fighting, bull fighting, they won't let me in."

I shook my head. It was unbelievable, but that's the government for you.

"If my country needed me, I'd go to the front lines tonight."

A lot of guys sat around camp fires at night and told lies, Nick Nagy told the truth.

I went to bed around two am on Saturday night. From what I hear Nick stayed up till four. When I dragged my ass to breakfast at eight am, mumbling the word "coffee" to anyone in ear shot, I noticed Nick doing farm work.

"Aren't you going to have breakfast?" I asked him.

"Finished it about an hour ago."

"You bull fighting again today?"

"Yep."

"What are you doing?" He was carrying around some concrete blocks.

"Working."

"Yeah, but, I didn't know you worked here on the farm too."

"I don't. I just seen some work that needed done; thought the Muxlow's could use a hand, so I got up early."

He walked away, concrete block in each hand, as I continued my pursuit of coffee.

That morning we ate our breakfast then the guys bucked some more bulls while I worked on my notes. By lunchtime the few remaining riders had had enough, and bull riding camp was essentially over.

"Remember," Gary told us, "the day you need a drink or a smoke of something funny to get on a bull is the day you better quit bull riding. I've seen guys lose everything they had cause of crystal meth and all that other crap. You have to separate yourselves from the losers. The adrenaline and the endorphins that your body pumps through you is enough of a high. I got a standing ovation from ninety thousand people! Ain't too many people in the world who will ever understand what that's like, but I'm telling you, it's a natural high and you can't beat it. You think positive, you live positive, and you're gonna be a winner."

I packed up my stuff and shook hands all around. The truth is I was sad to be leaving. After only three days I felt like a lot of these guys were my friends. Tim and Nate told me I could come and stay at the farm anytime I wanted to. We kept talking and the day grew later and later, they bugged me to stay one more night, but it was time for me to get on the road. Eventually I got into my Mustang, put the top down, and slowly rolled down the driveway.

"Hey!" Orie called to me. "You were good."

I nodded at him and smiled. He wasn't just an ordinary fifteen-year-old boy, he was a cowboy.

Afterword:

If you've read my bio, you know that I am an independent movie producer. I want to make Be Tough: The Caleb Griffin story, into my next film. An inspirational sports story, like Rudy, about a bull rider with one leg. I had dinner with Caleb last night and he's on board. I'm looking for sponsors. If you own a business and you're interested, or if you have any way to help us, please feel free to reach out to me at JPReisig@yahoo.com

THEY HAD AN ALLIGATOR, SO I WRESTLED IT.

I drove south through Florida and checked into the Everglades International Hostel. I had developed a chill during the car ride, and a very slight headache. Even though it was barely afternoon I thought it would be best if I took a short nap. I put my bag away and crawled into my bunk.

I opened my eyes, it was dark. The room was full of snoring people. The entire day had passed. People had come in and out, and I had not noticed. I had been "napping" for seven or eight hours. There would be no way that I would be able to sleep tonight.

I fell back to sleep.

I looked at my phone. It said 3. I could not figure out if it was 3 am or 3 pm. I rolled and moaned with pain. My sheets were all wet, I had sweated through everything. I had sold my father's house without his permission. My parents would have to move out. I panicked! I fell back to sleep.

It's four now, my phone says that it's four in the morning. No, it's not. There are new people in the room, there is light coming in from the windows, it is four pm, in the afternoon.

I force myself out of bed so I can pee and fill my water bottle. I should sit outside. I should try to eat something. I'm too tired. I just need a little nap. I crawl back into bed and sleep.

It is night now, the room is full, people are snoring. I have to leave. I have to find my keys. Today is draft day, I promised the coach I would be there to see which NBA team I will play for. I am too hot. I am too cold. I sleep.

I wake. I know who I am and where I am. I do not know what day it is or how long I have been lying here. I force myself out of bed and out of the hostel. The Quick Mart is one block away. I pull on my shoes.

I enter the quick mart. I realize I am not wearing pants. I have on an old T shirt, baseball cap, socks, running shoes, and a pair of sweat soaked boxer briefs. I stand there for a moment, asking myself if I care. I do not.

I bring a can of unsweetened apple sauce to the counter.

"Bayer" I say to the man. The store is full of the neighborhood bums buying liquor and lotto. I look worse than any of them.

"Guy? You ok guy?"

"Bayer." He hands me a sample pack containing a total of two pills. "You're killing me Mohammad. Get me the big bottle."

"Sure guy."

I stumble back to the hostel, walking the block in my sweaty boxer shorts. I need pills.

It's open. The Bayer is open. The safety cap is broken and the cotton is gone. I'm too weak to swear. I pull some shorts on and stumble back to the quick mart.

"I give you open bottle guy."

"Yeah."

"I think to myself; I give him a bottle that I used."

"Yeah."

"Here you go guy." He hands me a new bottle.

I take the Bayer. I drink some water. I fall into my bunk. I am so tired. I sleep.

I wake. It is 8pm now, but what day is it? I honestly don't know. How long have I been lying in the bunk? Two days? Or was it three? I don't know.

I step outside for the first time, entering the hostel's courtyard. I have seen nothing of the Everglades. I haven't even seen the hostel.

It's nicely done. Collections of tents, ropes and bridges leading to hammocks high up in the trees, Christmas lights everywhere.

"Hey! We thought you might be dead!" A hippy with ripped shorts and dreadlocks waves to me.

"Nope." I wave back. "And thanks for checking on me you bunch of New Age pricks," I think to myself.

Say what you will about Fox News Christians. Call them self-righteous, annoying, pushy, and I'd be inclined to agree with you, but here's a fact: they would not have left me to die in a hostel bunk. It may have been terribly annoying, and not at all helpful, to have a middle-aged woman praying with one hand in the air and the other on my forehead, but she would have made the effort. I promise you that a woman from the Midwest would have canceled her day of hiking so she could spoon feed me soup. Good luck finding a so-called peace and love socialist who will do that for a stranger.

I eat the can of applesauce.

I walk back to the Quick Mart.

"You look like you are shits, huh guy?"

"I'm a little better." I place two cans of chicken soup on the counter.

"Fuck me guy."

"Yeah." I look around. "I'll take one of those bananas too."

"You should have some chicken soup guy."

"Yeah."

"You need to take care of youself, you know?"

I sit in the hostel's courtyard and slowly eat a bowl of chicken soup and a banana. It is my first food in three days. Then I just sit. Around eleven I take some more Bayer and crawl back into bed. I sleep another nine hours.

When I wake I am feeling much better. Not good, but better, I'd say I am at 50%. Normally that would mean that I'm miserable, but in comparison to the previous days it was glorious.

I pulled on some shorts and walked around the corner.

"My number one guy! How are you today my friend?"

"Morning, Mohammad, a bit better."

"You need rest guy."

"I just slept about sixty hours in a row, I need food." I put a yogurt and a granola bar on the counter.

"I like you guy; you know what you body needs. Not like the fat peoples who shop at my store, look at these fat peoples." He sweeps his hand around in disgust at his customers.

I went back to the hostel, ate, then sat writing. It really was a nice hostel. The courtyard was more or less a well-groomed jungle. A canopy of trees shaded the entire area while chairs, tents, hammocks, and nooks were built everywhere for lounging and reading. There was even a hammock thirty feet up in the trees with a solid and safe path of rope ladders and bridges leading you up.

After I finished my breakfast, I decided that I might feel better if I took a shower. I have to say, of all the places I have been in the world I never expected a hostel in the Everglades to have one of the nicest showers I've ever been in, but it did.

The shower was outside. Walls surrounded all four sides, but there was no ceiling. The walls were all lined with naturally growing jungle plants, giving the impression that I was simply standing in the middle of the Florida tropics somewhere, having stumbled upon a shower. It really did feel like I was standing in warm rainwater on a beautiful outdoor day, which, I guess I was.

Around noon I was out of things to do. My breakfast was over, my writing was done, I had taken a shower. I didn't feel great, but I didn't feel terrible either. Being an American male, I figured this was good enough. I had come to see the Everglades; let's see the damn Everglades. I pulled my shoes on and got into the car.

GPS didn't work here, so I drove according to the directions the hostel receptionist gave me. As instructed, I came to a big farmer's market named Robert Is Here. I decided to stop and have a look around.

The first thing I noticed was that there was nobody there, besides me, who could possibly be named Robert. I was the only pale face. I looked like a Nordic giant. Not surprisingly the market was full of Spanish speakers. My mind always jumps to Mexicans, but given that this was South Florida they were probably mostly Cuban.

I wandered behind the market. Here they had a parrot in a cage, mini cows, burrows, a ram, and a big man with no shirt handling all the food.

Then I started to hear another language, and I saw another type of face entirely – Seminole Indians. Indians! Real Indians! Like from movies and history and stuff! There just simply aren't that many Native Americans in America, which, as I think about it, means there simply aren't that many anywhere. Once a year Detroit has a huge Thanksgiving Day parade. It's easy to round up a bunch of guys who look like my Uncle Tom to play the pilgrims, but good luck finding enough Indians. They always stick a couple of real Indians upfront, then fill in the background with a bunch of Puerto Ricans, a couple of Chinese kids, and a random Mexican in an Indian head dress.

The word "Seminole" is derived from the Muscogee word simanó-li, which may itself be derived from the Spanish word ci-marrón, meaning "runaway" or "wild one"

Originally part of the Creek tribe, the Seminole became increasingly independent of other Creek groups and established their own identity. They developed a thriving trade network during the British and second Spanish periods (roughly 1767–1821). The tribe expanded considerably during this time and, during the late 18th century, was further supplemented by free blacks and escaped slaves who became known as Black Seminoles.

The Seminole were first confined to a large inland reservation by the Treaty of Moultrie Creek and then forcibly evicted from Florida by the Treaty of Payne's Landing. By 1842, most Seminoles and Black Seminoles had been removed to Indian Territory west of the Mississippi River with perhaps fewer than 200 Seminoles remaining in Florida.

Today, the Seminole People have fostered a resurgence in traditional customs and a culture – as the new owners of The Hard Rock Café and Casinos!

I jumped back in my car. I was hungry for lunch now, a good sign. But where should I go? I typed restaurant into my phone. It spat back a bunch of places I couldn't pronounce, and a Denny's.

I happen to love Denny's. It was the favorite restaurant of my grandfather. It was my go-to joint in college. I wanted Denny's.

But I just couldn't do it. I'm on a trip to see America, not to eat at Denny's. So, I just drove for a mile to see what I would pass. The first thing I saw was the R@T Mini Mart. I'm sure that Roberto and Miguel thought that shortening their store's name from Roberto and Miguel's Mini Mart was a great idea, but they really should have run it by an English speaker first. Nobody wants to shop at the Rat Mart.

Next door was a little mom and pop Mexican joint. Mexican might not be the best idea, I thought to myself, but there were no other options. I could either have local or Denny's, I went local.

"Hola" a girl said to me as I walked in. Everyone spoke in Spanish. The menu was completely in Spanish. Man, this is weird. I went through the menu and simply looked at the pictures. They obviously specialized in three things, rice, beans, and The Virgin Mary.

I ordered the first two, and some grilled meat. When it came, I wolfed it down, chugged some water, paid my bill, shoved a few napkins in my pocket, and left.

Man, I felt great.

I drove past Robert Is Here again and headed towards the entrance to the Everglades national park. I passed a sign that was simply a big picture of a panther crossing the road. Then another sign warned me not to leave the road because of alligators. Soon, a third sign informed me not to pick up hitch hikers because there is a prison ahead. All three signs could have been combined telling me to stay the hell in my car. Panthers, alligators, and prisoners - this is not an ideal place for a flat tire.

When I got to the park I was once again surrounded by white people. Old, fat, white people from the Midwest. I had news for the owners of that fruit market: Robert wasn't there, Robert was here.

Everglades National Park is the third-largest national park in the contiguous United States after Death Valley and Yellowstone. Most national parks preserve unique geographic features; Everglades National Park was the first created to protect a fragile ecosystem.

The Everglades are a network of wetlands and forests fed by a river flowing just a quarter mile per day, out of Lake Okeechobee, southwest into Florida Bay. The park is the most significant breeding ground for tropical wading birds in North America and contains the largest mangrove ecosystem in the Western Hemisphere. Thirty-six threatened or protected species inhabit the park, including the Florida panther, the American crocodile, and the West Indian manatee, along with three hundred and fifty species of birds, three hundred species of fresh and saltwater fish, forty species of mammals, and fifty species of reptiles. The majority of South Florida's fresh water, which is stored in the Biscayne Aquifer, is recharged in the park.

The park was established in 1934, to protect the quickly vanishing Everglades.

I parked the car, swigged some water, and set out on the boardwalk. The path I chose was the shortest and easiest, a boardwalk over the wetlands that seemed to loop for about a mile. No chance of me ending up sick and exhausted in the middle of the jungle all night, this would be just a short amble through the park.

As I walked the boardwalk, I realized that I was too hot. Not just too hot like everyone out here was too hot, I had a fever and it was rising. I looked around. A sign told me I was .4 of a mile into my one-mile loop, there was no sense in turning around. I found a little patch of shade and a bench to sit on, rested there for five minutes, then pushed on.

I hadn't seen anything by the way. I mean I saw a few turtles, some birds, and a couple of really large bugs, but I was here for the big show! Show me a gator so I can go home and have a nap.

I walked on. That's when I felt it. Mexican food, making a comeback. I panicked. I was now .6 of a mile into my one-mile walk and I needed a toilet. I needed a toilet now, not in .4 of a mile, now! I walked a bit faster, but that made the situation worse. I slowed my walk way down. I clenched my butt way up. These two things helped yet they only delayed the problem. What they did not do is bring me quickly to a toilet.

I looked over the side. I didn't see any gators down there. I could scurry over the side, stand in water up to my ankles, and have a Mexican movement while hoping not to get bitten by a gator. No, I would not be doing that. In the grand scheme of things, it is better to shit yourself than be eaten by a gator.

I walked on; I made another fifty yards. Fifty yards was a real struggle, I could not do nearly half a mile, I just couldn't! I looked left, I looked right, the boardwalk twisted and turned so I could only see, and be seen, for a short distance. The good news was there was nobody around me, the bad news was, Mr. Rogers and his family could mosey around a corner at any moment. It didn't matter.

The shorts came down and I had a fast explosion on the boardwalk. Quickly I fished the napkins out of my pocket, put them to use, then yanked my shorts back up. The whole operation didn't last more than twenty seconds, but it had left some damage. Guiltily I looked left, looked right, then scurried off.

I took the two napkins and threw them over the side. I am against littering, especially in a national park, it's just that I'm a little more against walking around holding a piece of paper that's soaked with my own wet shit.

As I drove back I felt a slight headache, chills, and annoyance that I hadn't seen a single gator in the entire Everglades. I had managed to do nothing on this leg of my trip except take a loose shit on a boardwalk. Hardly a tale for the grandkids.

I came to a four way stop sign. Forward brought me to the prison. Left took me back to the hostel. Right said that would dead end, in three miles, at The Alligator Farm. I sat there for a few minutes, forehead sweating despite the AC running. then turned right.

"Screw it, show me a damned gator!"

"What do jou vant to essee?" The little girl with the thick accent asked me. So far all I'd seen were a bunch of chickens wandering loose around their parking lot.

"I don't know, whatever. What do you got?"

"It's ….. por the gator, y mas …. Por the air boato and jou vant the esshow too, yes?"

"Sure, the whole thing." I gave her twenty dollars. She gave me back a map, tickets to a gator wrestling show, a coupon for the gift shop, and a ticket for the air boat ride.

I walked through the lobby and into the roadside attraction.

America's roadside attraction era was the 1940s and 50s. The country was booming. The average middle-class family could afford a car, and they had time for vacations.

The highway system wasn't set up yet, so families would travel from small town to small town, visiting new stores, trying new foods, hearing new accents.

There's only so long that you can sit in one of those old hunks of American metal without stretching your legs, and soon entrepreneurs learned that they could buy cheap land in the middle of nowhere, but along side the highway, and set up a soda shop, diner, and entertainment.

Trained bears, giant slides, a forest full of plastic dinosaurs, UFO museums, the world's largest ball of twine, the Jolly Green Giant, haunted houses, underground taverns, and in Florida, alligator shows.

Feeling around fifty percent, I entered the attraction.

Right away, first thing I saw was a panther in a cage. I have no idea if places like this need a zoo license, but I can tell you this, they really make you appreciate places like The Detroit Zoo a lot more. It may not be ideal for a troupe of chimpanzees to only have a four-acre exhibit but it's a hell of a lot better than a cage.

But there it was, a panther. Ok, I thought, I've seen something.

Next, I walked by the croc pit. There they were, twenty or so crocs. Lying around, jaws open, looking back at me. Fine. I've seen them. I moved on.

"The air boats will be leaving in five minutes." The voice on the loudspeaker told us.

Air boats. That didn't seem like a good idea. Yet there in my pocket was a ticket. I mean I've already paid for the darn thing. I took a deep breath. I was feeling alright, not great, but ok. Maybe the gentle salt breeze in my face would be nice?

I loaded onto the boat and a man handed me ear protection, the type that professionals use to mow the lawn. "It's going to be noisy and it's going to be wet!"

Well, I thought, I have the earmuffs for the noise. I may be feeling ill, but a little water couldn't hurt me. And after all, I had paid for the ticket already.

I took an inside seat, put my earmuffs on, and got ready to go.

"Excuse me!" I looked around, seeing a fat woman on the dock waving her arms at me. I could barely hear her. "Excuse me!" I pulled off my earmuffs. "Would you mind trading seats with me? I want to sit on the inside, so I don't get all wet."

I thought to myself "I don't want to get all wet either lady." But being a man, I nodded and hopped out of the boat so she could take my middle seat.

Now I'm not one of those who foolishly believes that men and women are the exact same. I help women lift their suitcases into the overhead compartment on the airplanes. That makes sense to me. I am physically stronger and taller than a woman is. This did not make sense to me. Why couldn't she get wet? My larger bone structure and muscles do not repel water. I also didn't like how this "you're a man so you should suffer" arrangement only seemed to work one way. Let's say I had a hole in my socks, why can't I just run up to any woman on the street and ask her to mend them for me? It never works that way does it?

Regardless, I got out of the boat, then I helped her into the boat, which was no small feat as she was easily two hundred lbs., then I got back into her, now my, less desirable seat.

"Ok riders! It's going to be loud, it's going to be wet, and oh yeah…" The toothless man grinned as he pulled away from the dock "…it's going to be rough! That's right, we're going to be doing some 360 spins at forty miles per hour!" Everyone cheered. Everyone except me.
As we pulled out, I saw an alligator. Or a crocodile. I didn't know which it was, but I saw one in the wild! In the Everglades! I was happy. We could turn around now.

The man sped the boat up and my worries went away. The wind in my face felt great. This was very pleasant. Then he spun the boat and my shorts and shoes were instantly soaked with water. I looked at the lady to my right, she was nice and dry. Then he spun the boat a few more times and I threw up in her lap. Turns out I still had a little Mexican food left.

Back on dry land I stuck my head in the water fountain then filled up my bottle. It was probably time to get back in the car and drive back to the hostel, but my shorts were soaking wet and could use a few minutes in the sun, besides how hard could it be to sit and watch an alligator wrestling show? And after all, I had paid for the ticket.

The show started with a guy spouting off some facts about alligators and crocodiles that nobody in the audience heard, cared about, or remembered. I tried to grab a few. They can live to be a hundred years old, grow up to twenty feet, and they generally don't attack humans.

I didn't care for this last fact. The word generally doesn't work for me. Take chipmunks for example. We have some of those in the backyard. I'm not afraid to walk through the back-yard. You know why? Because I can say that chipmunks do not attack humans. I do not have to say that chipmunks generally do not attack humans. See the difference there?

After we heard some facts, the man pulled out a gator. Even to my untrained eye he seemed to be pushing the hundred-year-old mark, the gator that is, not the man. The gator hissed at the man; the man jumped on his back! Then the man pushed the beasts mouth shut, picked its head up, and tucked the gator's head under his chin.

I had two thoughts. One, this is exceedingly stupid! Two, I wonder if I could do this?

Three days later I was rested up, totally healthy, and nervous as hell. It was an understandable feeling; today I was going to be doing some alligator wrestling.

Like most things, alligator wrestling was born out of necessity. Southeastern Native Americans hunted alligators as a food source for thousands of years.

For tribes like the Seminole and Miccosukee, learning how to "handle" the reptiles was part of their existence. "We had to live off whatever Mother Nature provided us in the Everglades. We'd eat the tail, the meaty part. Later on, when the alligator skin had a value, we would hunt and skin the gators and bring the skin to trading posts and trade for things we couldn't grow." -Max Osceola, Seminole tribal councilman.

Later, in the 40s and 50s, alligator wrestling became a popular roadside attraction in the Florida region. Natives would put on shows while men like my grandfathers would stand too close, cigarette dangling from their mouth, waiting for their wife to snap off a photo. A gator would hiss and they'd spin, holding up the big right hand of justice, in case they had to John Wayne their way out of the situation.

So, here I was to take part in an ancient Seminole tradition, born from necessity, kept relevant by stupidity.

I shook hands with Josh, holding his hand long enough to do a quick digit count. I was relieved to see that the hand contained three fingers and a thumb, that's 80% of what he was born with, not bad for a man that wrestles alligators for a living! Still, I would have felt better with a trainer who had all of his fingers.

"I can't help but notice you're missing a finger." I said to him.

"Yep."

"I suppose that happens when you wrestle alligators?"

"I was landscaping, I cut this finger off with a chain saw."

"No shit? I'm actually really happy to hear that." I grinned. Josh gave me an odd sideways glance.

"Well, you ready to see some gators?"

Josh showed me to the gator pit. Let's just say I wasn't looking forward to jumping in. There had to be about fifteen grown gators in there, most of them silently looking at me with their mouths open. They're an ugly creature that just doesn't seem to fit in with modern life.

The name "alligator" is probably an anglicized form of el lagarto, the Spanish term for "the lizard", which early Spanish explorers and settlers in Florida called the alligator. Eary English spellings of the name included allagarta and alagarto.

An average adult alligator weighs eight hundred pounds and is thirteen feet long. When standing near one it can be measured in a slow but steady exhale followed by someone mumbling "F me." The largest ever recorded measured a bit over nineteen feet.

Gators tend to live between thirty-five and fifty years. We do know that a few have past the eighty-year mark in captivity.

Alligators first appeared during the Oligocene epoch about thirty-seven million years ago. In other words, they're a dinosaur that forgot to die off.

They're one of the very few remaining creatures that don't quite understand that humans are on the top of the food chain.

My Uncle Tom and my Aunt Sue recently retired to Hilton Head. They love the weather, the golf, the ocean, but they're afraid to let their little dog Sammy off the leash least he get eaten by an alligator. In addition to eating our dogs, cats, and other things that are under the protection of humans, gators sometimes have the chutzpah to come after us! Every now and again a friend will email me a video of an old man in checkered pants dropping his clubs and running for his life back to his little golf cart! Well there wouldn't be any running from gators today. I was here now, and I was here to wrestle a gator!

"The first thing you got to understand," Josh said to me, "is if you're going to handle alligators, sooner or later you're going to get bit."

"How many times have you been bit?"

"Once or twice."

"What do you mean once or twice? See this makes me angry, it's like talking to a new girlfriend. You didn't sleep with one or two guys and you can't remember; you know exactly what your number is. Now, how many times have you been bit?"

"Three times."

I exhaled deeply and loudly.

"Don't worry about it." He said. "People only get bit if they want to get bit."

"Who the hell would want to get bit?"

"See the thing is, most people don't know how to behave around a wild predator. You got to be the alpha male. Let's say a gator charges you right? What are you going to do?"

"I'm going to get the hell out of Dodge."

"And that's exactly what you don't want to do. You got to stand your ground. See ninety nine percent of the time that any wild animal charges, it's just a bluff."

"Yeah, it's the one percent of the time that worries me. You know when you go to Vegas you have about a forty nine percent chance of winning, but the house has a fifty one percent chance. In the end, the house always wins."

"You ever seen The Hangover?"

"Yeah."

Josh went silent then. For about a full minute I waited for him to make some sort of analogy.

"You were saying?"

"What?"

"About The Hangover."

"Yeah."

"What about it?"

"Huh?"

"What about The Hangover?"

"I just like that movie."

We went back to staring at the gator pit for a few minutes. I wasn't sure why I was doing this. I was sure that if a gator charged me, I had no intention of standing my ground.

"So." I said. "Want to teach me some gator wrestling?"

"Oh we don't wrestle gators."

"What?" Then what was I doing here?

"No, too many protesters. Hippies, liberals, homos, that sort of thing."

"So..."

"No, we handle alligators."

"What?" I pulled out my smart phone and pulled up his website. "Learn the art of alligator wrestling!"

"Well, I don't know anything about that."

"So, what is alligator handling?"

"It's the exact same thing."

"But more acceptable to the homos?"

"Exactly. You ready?"

"Ready as I'm going to get."

I stood in a kiddie swimming pool. Josh held a two-foot-long baby alligator with his mouth taped shut. Part of me was relieved, part of me was humiliated.

He explained to me the proper way to catch a gator. "Gators bump into stuff with their tail all the time, branches and other junk in the river, so lightly hitting their tail doesn't make them jump or even turn. So as long as you grab their tail lightly, they won't even think about it."

"Ok." The little baby gator swam circles around me. I was beginning to wonder how good Josh was at applying tape. If that mouth came open it may not rip my leg off, but it would sure hurt.

"Once you have the tail, drag them backwards. They don't know what's happening so instead of spinning they'll try to move forward. Once you have them back by your front knee, jump on their back and put all of your weight on him."

"On the baby?"

"No, we're just using him to practice. I have a seven-footer in the bag for you."

"Seven feet?"

"Yeah."

"But I'm not even six feet! I'm 5'10!"

"With the little guy just get used to snatching him by the tail."

"And what do you mean you have a seven-foot gator in the bag? What are you doing walking around with an alligator in a bag?"

After an hour of snatching and grabbing the little guy, Josh brought out the bag. I was still standing in the kiddie pool when a seven-foot gator slid its way in there with me.

I've been in pools before with some people who I'd rather not share a pool with. People who looked like they hadn't showered in weeks. Guys with extremely hairy backs. I once had to get out of a pool because a little kid had taken a crap and it was now floating around. This gator was the worst thing I had ever been in a pool with.

"Is its mouth shut!"

"Yeah."

"You got its mouth taped shut?"

"Yeah."

"You're sure?"

"Yeah."

"Did you double tape it? Sometimes I go to the grocery store and they don't double bag. The groceries just fall out all over the parking lot."

"It's taped."

"Cause if it's a matter of saving money I'll pay for the extra tape."

"Ok, just lightly grab his tail and pull him back."

I grabbed him by the tail, just as Josh said, he tried to move forward. I pulled him back then pounced on his back!

"Now forearms on the top of his snout. If his mouth wasn't taped it would be time to push it closed."

I put my forearms on the top of the gators nose and pretended to push it shut.

"Now transfer your hands, one at a time, to hold his mouth closed."

I did.

"And finally raise his head up. When its head goes back the gator will become relaxed and go to sleep."

"Just like my father."

I went through the routine another twenty times over the next three or four hours. I felt like it was becoming easy.

"So." Josh looked at me. "I hear you want to try one with the mouth open."

"Yep!" I shot it out as quickly as I could, before I had any chance to change my mind.

Josh hopped into the water. He quickly trapped the gator, pinned it down, and removed the tape. The beast opened his jaws and hissed, slashed around, then hissed again. I stood twenty feet back from the pool.

"When was he fed last?"

"He's not hungry. He's just a bit upset right now."

I thought that being upset, from the gator's standpoint, was reasonable. To begin, he had started his day out in a bag. Who knows how long he was in there? Next, he was put into a shallow pool, had his mouth taped shut, and had an idiot from the Midwest wrestling him for the last four hours. Still, reasonable or not, I did not like the looks of an upset alligator.

"Why don't we give him a few minutes?" Josh suggested.

"Sure."

"So, what else have you done?"

"Huh?"

"I heard you drove in a demolition derby?"

"I don't know, yeah, maybe, I don't remember. So, you said you've been bitten three times."

"Yeah, but I've been doing this for a long time."

"Why would you think that would make me feel better? But you still have all your fingers?"

"Well not the…"

"Not the chain saw one, right."

"Yeah. I think he's ready. Want me to give him a go first?"

"Yeah. Yeah, that sounds like a good… Go ahead."

So Josh walked forward to the kiddie pool. Less than a minute later he was on the gator's back with its jaw pressed shut. "Ok, I'm going to let him go, then it's your turn. Just do it like we've been doing all morning, ain't nothing changed."

I ought to change my shorts, I thought to myself. Josh pushed the gator left and exited the pool to the right.

"Ok, dude, your turn."

"Yeah." I stood there and looked at the pool.

"I'm right here."

"You're right where?"

"Here."

"That's the side of the pool."

"Right here by the side of the pool for you."

"Uh huh."

"I got the stick."

"What exactly are you going to do with that stick anyway?"

"If he bites you, I'll pry his jaws open."

"Oh good."

I inched my way towards the pool, carful to stand directly behind the gator. Alligators have very good peripheral vision, but they can't see behind them or directly in front of them.

The gator splashed his tail and I backed up four feet in one step.

"It's alright. Go on."

"I'll go at my own pace. You just…"

I stepped gingerly into the water, careful not to make the slightest of ripples. First one foot, then the next.

"Hey look who's in the pool!" Josh laughed. I wanted to tell him to shut up, and worse, but I might need him and his stick in a minute.

I slid forward a bit. I was now way too centered in the pool for comfort. It would not be one easy step to dry land; the edge was now two or three big steps away. I did not like that.

"Slowly grab his tail."

I reached down with my right hand and took a hold of his tail, then, like I had practiced all morning, I ripped it back like I was starting a lawn mower and pounced on the animal's back!

I felt him fight me underwater. I plunged my face under the surface so I could put my chest and all of my weight on the beast! I pinched my knees extremely tight! I would not let him roll and shake me!

In less than three seconds he had given up. His mouth was wide open and hissing loudly, but I controlled his body.

"Now use your forearms to press his mouth closed."

I pressed my weight down even harder. I am 172 lbs. I'm pretty proud of this. I'm as strong as the average 195 lbs America; I just don't carry around the extra twenty pounds of beer and pizza fat. Right now, I was wishing I weighed over two hundred.

I moved my left forearm up and across his snout, then joined it with my right one. Alligators are very strong at biting down on something, like, for example, me, but they have very little muscle to keep their mouths open. Apparently when God was designing them it never occurred to Him that some stupid monkey would jump on their backs and try to force their mouths shut. I pushed down with both forearms and soon its mouth was pressed closed.

"Ok, now control the mouth by transferring your hands to the sides and holding the mouth shut."

This is how people lose hands; I thought to myself, this is why Josh has a stick.

I kept his mouth shut by keeping pressure on its snout with my right forearm, then transferred my left hand to the left side of the gator's mouth and held on tightly.

"Ok. Now this is the toughest part. You have to quickly move your right hand from holding the snout down, to grabbing the right side of its mouth."

Why? I thought to myself. Why do I have to do that? I could have boarded a cruise boat and been drinking rum out of a coconut right now.

"Just remember," Josh went on, "if you miss the grab, get both of your hands out of the way, but maintain control of the body."

I took a deep breath then shot my hand off of the snout and around to the right side of the mouth. I had it! I had the gator by both sides of its mouth!

I tilted the beasts head back, further and further, until finally I felt the gator relax and go out. He was mine now. I placed his head under my chin, put my hands out to my sides, and posed for pictures.

"Let's go again!" I was excited now, I felt great.

Josh let the gator back into the water. I slowly and silently stepped into the pool and crept up behind him. I reached down and lightly grabbed his tail with my left hand, then pulled him back. As soon as I did I felt a sharp pain in my wrist!

When I went all the way across the track in the derby, and crashed into that station wagon, I had jammed my wrist on the steering wheel. This was the same left wrist that I had already injured bull riding. The wrist was still only at fifty percent. I tried to hold on but I could not! The tail came loose, and the gator spun!

I'll tell you what I didn't do, I didn't stand my ground! Teeth flew near me; I jumped back then cleared the hell out of the pool!

Here's a bit of wisdom for you:

"Never go alligator wrestling if you just fractured your wrist bull riding then hurt it again in a demolition derby." -Joel Paul Reisig

I think I'll send that quote to the US Copyright Office. I can have it framed and sold at the Hobby Lobby.

"You alright?" Josh yelled to me.

"Yep."
"Want to go again?"
"Nope."

THE MAN IN
THE ARENA

The following is a true story, based solely on one unreliable source: my memory. All of the events happened over ten years ago. I had no intention of writing about it, took no notes, and was hit in the head multiple times.

The majority of the names have been changed, if not forgotten, and composite characters have been formed.

A few of the characters have become moderately famous. Through my acting and comedy, I interacted with guys who would go on to have film/TV careers. Through boxing I interacted with men who would become somewhat known to the sporting world, including one who is now in the UFC Hall of Fame. They are not major characters, and I have left their names alone.

Finally, I understand that there are a decent number of passages in this story that can be considered racist. Standup comedian's jokes are often based on their own race and identity. Boxing was, and is, a tribal sport. Chicago is a very diverse city, but that does not mean it is a mixed city. Racism was common at the fights; the crowds picked their favorites based on who looked like them. The gyms naturally kept not only to their own styles of boxing, but to "their own people" as well. In the city at night, racism fell out of my Italian friend Gino's mouth without him ever realizing it. Rylan Worth, my comic friend, had no problem calling out all the no talent hacks that relied solely on their identity to form jokes. At my day job, the "real whites" felt superior to the Polish, the Polish distrusted the blacks, who more or less hated everybody. The blacks were ok with me though because I was half

Jewish and thus not really white. I've decided not to shy away from these realities.

Had I kept complete notes years ago I'm sure I could make this chapter of my life into a full book. As is, I hope that I am able to dust off enough old memories to bring you an entertaining and interesting short story.

"You serious?"

The trainer looked at me. Everyone in the gym looked at me. The popping noise of gloves against heavy bags stopped. A few guys in the background laughed.

"Yeah, I'm serious."

"What is you?"

"I'm sorry?"

"You a Polish? Lots of white boys around here be Polish, some of them can fight too. But you don't look like no Polish."

"No."

"So what is you?"

"I don't..."

"You ain't black."

"No."

"You ain't no Mexican."

"No."

"So what is..."

"I'm Irish Jewish."

"Negro, is you Irish or is you a Jewish?"

"I'm half Iri... what difference does it make?"

"Man, what the hell you want to be a fighter for? You rich. Go home."

I turned towards the exit. A few guys snickered. Mitts started to pop off again. Then I spun, I had one more question for him.

"Hey! What are you? And don't tell me black cause you're probably half white, and on your African side you don't have the slightest idea what tribe you're from!"

He looked at me. "You think you's a fighter?"

"That's right."

"Alright. Let's get some gloves on you."

I stood in the ring of an all-black gym. Nobody was in my corner. The coach stepped into the ring as the referee. Across from me was a fighter, maybe 19 years old. They told me that he'd been training for a year and had two wins and one loss as an amateur. I was about 165 lbs, he looked similar.

"Alright, let's see."

A bell rang. We both came forward. I didn't know anything about boxing other than what I had seen on TV. I kept my gloves high. He threw a few punches which landed on my gloves, the impact coming through them and jarring my face.

I tried to throw a jab. When I did, he landed square on my nose.

They say you can tell who is a fighter, and who is not, the very first time they get hit. Some guys ball up, back away, quit entirely. They may become fantastic wrestlers later, football players, Hollywood stunt men, but they'll never be a boxer. Others get angry. When I got punched, I wanted to hit him back.

I charged forward with punches, landing very few, getting hit more often than not.

It went like this for three rounds. A round of professional boxing is three minutes long, amateur fights are two minutes but they often train in the gym with three-minute rounds. Doesn't sound like much, to those who have not done it.

At the end of three rounds, three minutes each, the coach asked us both if we wanted two more rounds. I said yes.

My opponent, who had won every round, said he was tired. His coach told him to tough it out, but he didn't. He quit.

"Let me see that nose kid." I had a nosebleed; the coach took care of it. "Where you stay at?"

"What?"

"You don't know where you stay fool?"

"Where do I live?"

"Yes, where does you live at?"

"Lincoln Park."

"Old Town ain't far from you. You want to go to Kahne's Konner. I'll call my friend Joe Kahne tonight and tell him you be coming by tomorrow. He train guys like you all the time. Won't be easy on you, he a good trainer, but it a white boy gym."

I came to Chicago to study comedy. That night, nose still dripping a little blood, I checked into my first class at the legendary Second City.

Chicago was and is the home of improvised comedy, better known as improv. Improv is the art of working with a team to step on stage, live, in front of a paying crowd, and perform; without having the slightest idea what it is that you will be performing.

Crowds flocked each weekend, and many weeknights, to the famous Second City Theater. This improv theater had been the training grounds for generations of the world's top comedic talent. Dan Aykroyd, Steve Carell, Tina Fey, John Belushi, John Candy, Bill Murphy, Amy Poehler, Mike Myers, Chris Farley, Tim Meadows, Stephen Colbert, Halle Berry, Amy Sedaris, Jon Favreau... I could keep this paragraph going forever. I wanted to be next on that list, the next with a photo on their wall.

In the long run it turned out that I liked pure standup, the art of taking on the audience all on my own, better than the teamwork of improv. Regardless, my improv training always proved helpful whether I was on stage for standup, improv, live theater, or in front of the camera in a film.

Here is the number one thing that improv taught me, that it teaches everyone: listen. Acting is not acting, it is reacting. Listen to the other person in your scene and react naturally to them. Do not hold a joke in your mind waiting to fire it off, listen to your acting partner and be funny, or serious, organically.

I also learned that if you walk into an improv class with a bloody nose, you have to answer a lot of questions.

Boxing, also called pugilism (literally fist fight), is likely one of the worlds two oldest sports, along with its counterpart;

running.

There is a clear evidence that boxing existed as early as 1500 BC, on Crete Island. Modern researchers insist that such duels had been known even earlier than that, in Africa, specifically in the region of modern Ethiopia. Hieroglyphic scriptures dating back to the year 4000 BC revealed the popularity of boxing throughout the Nile Plateau and all over Egypt. We know that boxing, along with the combat sport pankration, marathon, and a few equestrian sports, was a part of the original Olympics.

In the 1800s champions such as John L. Sullivan fought under the London Prize Rules. Bare knuckle fights with rounds that ended only when one fighter was knocked down.

In time we adapted the Marquess de Queensberry Rules that are still in effect today:

-Opponents to wear padded gloves

-The round lasted for three minutes of fighting, with a one-minute break required

-Any other kind of fighting except for using hands was forbidden

-Any of the boxers who touched the ring floor had to stand up within 10 seconds; otherwise he was claimed to be beaten and the fight proclaimed ended

I felt at home the first time I stepped into Kahne's Korner. Joe Kahne looked me over, then called out to his assistant coach, Mark.

"He looks like me, doesn't he?"

"He's good looking, you're old."

"Good hair, got those sharp features just like me. Looks like me when I was 25."

Mark came over and looked at me closer. Mark was in his mid-thirties, maybe forty. "He's got a big nose. You got a big nose."

"This is Mark. He's a pain in the ass but we love him."

"Train him good Joe, or that thing is going to get broke."

"Nah, we're not going to let you get hit kid. That Mexican style of boxing, hit and get hit, all the macho nonsense, that's stupid. This game is about hitting and moving. You watch Floyd Mayweather fight?"

"I've seen some of his fights."

"I want you to see all of them, multiple times. He under-stands the game. He hits, and he moves. That's what I'm going to teach you. Look kid, watch my feet, I pivot to the left and I let the opponent's right-hand roll gently off of my shoulder, then I pivot back and I hit him, then I step out and reset. Boxing's not about your hands, it's all about your feet. Mark, get him started."

Mark put me through two hours of footwork drills that night. At the end, Joe came back.

"Well?" He asked Mark.

"He listens. We can make a matador out of him."

Practice lasted from six to eight. When it was done, I showered at the gym, threw my shorts into my backpack, and hopped onto my bike.

I rode three miles north, to a club in Wrigleyville.

"Who are you here to see?" The guy at the door asked me.

"Huh?"

"Are you here to see anybody? If a comic brings a good crowd, we give him more time."

"No, um, I am a comic."

"You any good?"

"Yeah." I'm not sure if I lied. I'd never done standup com-edy before. But I was pretty sure that I would be good. I'd written an act, and I'd rehearsed it in the shower. I was really good at mak-ing speeches, like in front of a class, weddings, or other groups. I just sort of knew I could do this.

"Alright, I can get you on at 9:40. You get seven minutes. The red light comes on at six minutes, that means you got a minute to wrap it up. If you're still on the stage past eight minutes I cut your mic and you don't get invited back. Understand?

"Yeah. Thanks."

I stood there, in the doorway, awkwardly. He looked at me, wondering what the hell I was still doing there. Why was I still a part of his life?

"Yeah?"

"Um, how much?"

"How much what kid?"

"To get in?" I only had ten dollars with me, for the whole night.

"Thought you said you were a comic?"

"Yeah."

The conversation stopped again. I didn't talk. He didn't talk. For a few beats he just looked at me, like I was an idiot.

"So you walk in."

"Oh, um, right. Thanks."

Inside the club, I stood in the back, holding up a wall.

"You a comic?"

"Um, yeah."

"Well, sit down." A guy pushed back an empty seat. "This is the comic table."

So I joined the table of misfit toys. A slew of young white guys, a girl who wanted to prove that she could be crasser than any guy, fat black dudes, an old guy in a tuxedo for no reason, a woman with a ventriloquist dummy, and Rylan Worth.

Rylan was in his mid-twenties but already terribly balding. He was skinny, yet his body was devoid of any muscle. He sank into his chair like he didn't have bones, his head flopped backwards, arms hanging like noodles as he looked at the ceiling and said "Make it stop.", in reference to the endless line of amateur comedians going on the stage.

"You Jewish?" A guy at the table asked me.

"I've been in this town for two days and that's all anyone has asked me. What difference does it make?"

"He's trying to figure out what hack jokes you're going to tell." Rylan told me. "There's not a single person at this table who can write a real joke."

"Here we go again." A forty-year-old women who called herself T-Squared rolled her eyes.

"Like Jim here is gay…"

"Heyyyyy."

"So he thinks anything gay is funny. And these audiences are so stupid that they actually laugh. And every single black guy in this club has one damn joke. Black people do this, white people do that..."

"If you're so good how come bookers aren't booking you?"

Rylan flopped back into his chair and went back to staring at the ceiling. "Because they're idiots. They're all a bunch of idiots."

"I just want to point something out." Was the first sentence I ever said on a standup comedy stage. One thing I hadn't counted on, I was blind. A huge light was aimed right at me, of course. It had never occurred to me that every time a comic looks out into the crowd, all he is really seeing is a wall of light. The rest, all the interaction, is just an act. He pretends that he can see you, and talks to you naturally, making you feel like he's actually looking at you.

"Here we are in Wrigleyville, the crowd is entirely white, except for one table of black people in the back." The room got quieter. "I just want to ask you. Where the hell is Rosa Parks when you need her?"

The table of black people erupted in laughter, giving the rest of the room permission to.

"You're good." Rylan sat at my table after my set. I was on a euphoric high that I have rarely felt before. It is how I imagine your first hit of crack cocaine must be. I wanted more.

"Thanks."

"I mean you stand too still, it made you look nervous, and your set ups are too long, also you need to go bluer, your stuff's too clean, and I heard that one joke before, about the wall, I'm not saying you stole it, it's just hack, any idiot can come up with that, but at least you didn't just do hack jokes, other than that one. These guys suck, I mean it, they all suck, but you had some good stuff like a real comic, you want to roll with me to Uptown Tavern?"

"What's that?"

"Another open mic. I mean it sucks, but it's stage time, right? These guys, they don't have any talent at all, but they're also all lazy. They get out and do one or two open mics a week and feel good about themselves. You got to work your material man. I do at least two sets every night, three if I can. Once, on a Saturday, I even did four, that's how you get good, you need stage time, you got a bike?"

"Yeah."

"So let's go."

We jumped on our bikes and rode a few miles through the endless traffic jams of a typical Chicago night. It was 11 pm, still early in America's 2nd city. There was a small line outside of Uptown Tavern when we arrived.

"Come on."

Rylan bypassed the line at the door and shook the bouncer's hand. "This is my friend Ben."

"Hey Ben." I said to the bouncer.

"Darrel."

"Huh?"

"Darrel."

"Who's Ben?"

"You're Ben." Rylan told me.

"Joel."

"Are you sure?"

"Quite."

"Whatever, he's a comic, he's actually not a hack."

The bouncer nodded and let us in, no handstamp, no ID, no cover charge.

That night was the first of many times that I got to witness Rylan work. On stage Rylan was without a doubt the best comic in the room. In the back of the room myself and the other comics died from laughter. His bits were genius.

But the audiences didn't always think so. Often they just looked at him.

Halfway through a bit, Rylan stopped. "You people are idiots, you're all a bunch of idiots, and I'm an idiot for thinking I can get you to understand what real comedy is! It's like I'm trying to teach a dog how to do trigonometry. The dog's not the idiot because he can't learn trigonometry. I'm the idiot for trying to teach a dog trigonometry! Do you even understand what I'm saying? You're the dogs!"

Even in his angry rant, he was hilarious. At the back of the room, the entire comic table laughed uncontrollably. Someone spit his Cherry Coke all over the table. Oh, that was another perk I was learning about tonight, comics got free fountain drinks, coffee, and pretzels.

Then, with half of his time remaining, Rylan walked off the stage. The MC raced back up as Rylan, still cursing, melted into the chair next to mine.

There were two more comics up before me. The first one started with a typical hack joke.

"I'm a gay Mexican. Ever wonder what a gay Mexican looks like? That's right, like a Chinese lesbian."

The crowd erupted in laughter.

From the back Rylan yelled "That?! You're laughing at that!?". Then he flopped over and lay his head on the table, his face in the spit up Cherry Coke. "I wish somebody would just shoot me."

After midnight we sat in a cheap Mexican taco place.

"I get dinner here every night. It sucks, but the tacos are only fifty-nine cents each, plus there's a penny bowl, so I order two, but I just bring a dollar and then I take eighteen pennies out of the bowl, it pisses the owner off, but what the hell does he care, they're just pennies, your bit about the dog, that was good."

By one am we were sitting in our third open mic comedy room of the evening.

This one was a comic's room. Meaning there really wasn't any crowd. Twenty-five comics filled the room, not ordering, not tipping, just watching each other and waiting for their turn to perform.

"You have to sit through about a hundred no talent hacks here, but I like the room, it's a comic's room so you can bring your notes right up on stage, I mean the place sucks, obviously, but you got to work your material."

I did. I had been writing a bit on phone sex and I decided that two am at a comic's room would be a perfect place to try it. Here was the basic idea:

"Now I'm smoothly taking your bra off with one hand. Ok, now I'm using two hands. Now I'm just yanking at the bra, trying to break this stupid metal clasp! Now you're pushing my hands away as you mumble 'idiot' under your breath…" And I continue to have phone sex, badly.

The room didn't really laugh, comics don't do that, but they nodded approvingly, and a few told me that I had something there.

At three am I rode my bike back to my studio apartment.

Joe Kahne's Korner was on the second floor of a typical fitness gym. We could use the treadmills and weights downstairs if we wanted, but very few of the guys did.

Our workouts started with the jump rope. That will blast your cardio, and build your legs, better than anything they had downstairs. For strength, we did push-ups, pull ups, sit ups, and we boxed. The longer I stayed, the leaner and stronger I became.

The guys downstairs, I honestly don't know what they were doing. Their workout consisted of two of the most worthless pieces of fitness equipment ever invented, the bench press and the squat. They grew bigger, less flexible, less endurance, less functionable. Our domain was upstairs, where the real workouts in the gym happened.

For months I trained hard. My two main training partners were Darrius, a Welsh fighter and former semi-professional rugby player who had bricks in both hands, and Luke "The Real" McCoy, a model who was constantly underestimated due to his good looks, but his opponents learned quickly that he could fight.

Luke of course was not the "real" Real McCoy. The nickname

originally belonged to boxer Charles "Kid" McCoy. McCoy was a middle weight, tall and slightly built. One evening he was minding his own business, having a beer, when a local tough bumped into him. Refusing to apologize, the man continued to provoke McCoy. When somebody told him that this was the boxer Charles McCoy, he laughed and challenged McCoy to a fist fight. This unassuming man couldn't be the fighter from the radio. Upon waking up on the floor a few seconds later, the man reportedly said, "My God, that was the real McCoy".

Luke McCoy, a professional model, did not have the look of a fighter, but he was also the real deal.

Darrius, "The Welsh Windmill", was the model of functionable strength. Prior to arriving in America, he played Rugby on a semi-professional level. Downstairs huge guys roamed from the bench press to the squat racks. At 5'8 and a very solid 185 lbs, there wasn't a man down there that Darrius couldn't polish off in thirty seconds. He could move, hit hard, move again, hit harder, and keep it up all day.

Luke didn't hit nearly as hard, but he was an athletic guy and he picked up the clean/professional style of boxing that Joe taught. He was tough to catch, and he could hit you from all angles.

Darrius fought at 168, Luke at 160. They both walked around about 12 to 15 lbs heavier, then cut to their fighting weights. My shape had improved in the past few months, and I entered the gym most days around 158 lbs now. Joe told me that when I started fighting it would be at 147. There were guys my size at the gym, and smaller too of course, but I enjoyed sparring with Luke and Darrius.

I got to chat often with Mike Starr, a big Italian guy who came in to hit the heavy bags and shoot the shit with Joe. Mike was a professional actor; you may remember him as the huge Italian guy who stood behind Robert DeNiro and looked tough. If you don't remember him in those movies, you may remember him from a bunch of other movies he did. In these, he stood behind Al Pacino and looked tough. Oh, he talked a little bit too, but mostly he just pushed a guy around when the mob boss told him to.

Our boxing team shared our upstairs space with another group. They were soft spoken, polite, and dangerous.

Joe split the upstairs with Carlson Gracie Senior, one of the most respected Brazilian Jujitsu coaches in the world.

Gracie Jujitsu was brought to America in 1992. The Gracie family started the Ultimate Fighting Championship, the UFC, to showcase their martial art to the world. In a series of no-rules matches, Royce Gracie, an unassuming man of 174 lbs, easily defeated much larger and more athletic opponents from all the various styles of martial arts.

Jujitsu is primarily a ground art, a form of wresting with the goal of putting your opponent into a choke hold or a joint lock. It is very effective.
Every day I would shadow box in the ring, while watching Mr. Gracie train his students.

Joe had great respect for him, and the other way around. Together they trained our gym's heavyweight, the champion of Chicago, Stephan Bonner.

The real star of the gym, Stephan was 6'4, 225 lbs, and the heavyweight amateur boxing champion of Chicago. Rumor had it that Dana White had his eye on him for a future contract with the UFC.

One day I was working the mitts with Mark. Double jab, slip the jab, slip the right, fire a right to the body, circle out, jab again. My footwork was getting great. My head movement felt slick.

"You got those fast hands kid." Joe said as he watched me from the ring. Behind him, Stephan paced like a hungry lion. "Hey, get in here!"

Mark lowered the pads. I jumped into the ring.

"Stephan has a fight with a speed demon coming up. Stephan, no power, just jabs. Throw some jabs at him, see if you can catch him."

I moved. Stephan threw and I slipped it to my right. He threw again and I stepped back. He double jabbed and I slipped them both.

Then all of a sudden a brick fell from the ceiling and hit

me in the forehead. That's not really what happened, but it may as well of been. I felt the force of Stephan's "light jab" all the way down my spine. I don't know how else to describe it. To this day I remember that he hit me in the forehead and the force of it transferred all the way down my spine to where my backbone connects to my tailbone.

Boxing has weight classes for a reason. Sure, I can fight with the typical American who is 190 lbs of bacon fat, but Stephan was 225 lbs of learn muscle. His shoulders were huge, his wrists were huge, his fists seemed double the size of mine. I'd sparred with Luke, who boxed at 160, without any problems. I sparred with Darrius, a power puncher at 168, slipping most of his punches but managing to handle the ones that did land. A full blown 6'4 American heavyweight was another animal.

"Nope." I said out loud, and for the first and only time in my life I crawled out of the ring mid round.

"I hate Tuesday nights." Rylan said to me as we rode our bikes downtown to the first of three open mics we would perform at tonight. "All the Tuesday night clubs suck."

Every time he talked I couldn't help but laugh. His wispy hair on his half bald head fell in every direction, his corduroy pants were always too long and dragging on the ground, and he never seemed be able to keep his shoes tied. Twice a night I'd stop and wait for him as he worked his shoelace out of his bike chain.

He wasn't wrong about Tuesday nights though. The first club literally had me standing on the bar, like a nineteen-year-old dancing girl, or some kind of top shelf liquor that could tell jokes. The second club was in Boy's Town. They drew a good-sized crowd, all male, and were more interested in looking at my fit boxer's body than anything I had to say. The third club had me standing under a TV, with sports replays of that week's games on mute, happening directly over my head. I had to try to fit quick jokes in-between exciting plays. There was also a pool table between me and the meager crowd. Every once in a while, a guy would walk by me, bend over, and cut my stage in half as his pool stick slid backwards while he lined up his shot.

But what the hell, it was stage time. Every set made you better.

On a Saturday night the team all gathered at the gym. But there would be no training tonight. We grabbed our gear and loaded into an old full-sized passenger van. Mark drove, Joe sat in the passenger seat telling him which routes to take. We were on our way to South Chicago, to a rival gym.

Some of the guys smiled and laughed. Others, like me, were nervous. Tonight would be my first fight.

Gym Wars are different than usual events. Joe knew all the trainers at all the gyms, and he had an at least ok relationship with most of them. We piled out of the van and entered an old boxing gym. Mexican flags hung on the walls next to photos of Mexican fighters. Unlike our Northside gym, this was a stand-alone building, boxing only.

A few Mexican boys set up folding chairs, an old lady sold tickets for cash to the line outside the door, working class men smoked cigarettes in the back and appraised us.

One of their assistant coaches showed us to the girl's locker room, which would serve as the visiting team's locker room for tonight.

Next, one by one, their assistant coach watched us step on the scale. We were matched up against our counter parts on their team, Joe and their head coach both doing their best to match us against someone our own weight and experience.

We would all fight at our natural weights tonight, no weight cutting. The weigh ins happened only an hour before the fight, so there was no time for anyone to cut weight then rehydrate. I weighed 158 lbs.

They had a 157 lbs fighter, but Joe said no to me fighting him. He had over fifty amateur fights. Instead, Joe matched me against a 164 lbs fighter, it would also be his first match ever.

I pulled my gear on, then stepped into the gym to stretch and do a few light rounds with a jump rope.

Around the ring roughly a hundred folding chairs were set up. The crowd consisted of their friends, their family, their neighborhood. Spanglish was the only language spoken throughout the night, including the announcer and the referee.

The night started with a 112 lbs fight. We didn't have a fighter that small, so their 112 lbs fighter took on a new guy from our gym who was about ten pounds heavier. Next match was at 130 lbs, then another at 139 lbs.

Our team lost all three.

The lighter weight classes were the "Mexican weights". The vast majority of their gym naturally competed between 112 and 147. We didn't even have a 112 lbs fighter. Our lightest guy was 125 lbs, but a 125 undeveloped nineteen-year-old white kid is no match for a thirty-year-old Mexican man of the same weight.

This is when I learned something else about gym wars, they weren't "wars" at all. They weren't even quite "fights". They were events to help us get used to competing in front of a crowd, in a hostile environment, and against an opponent who was not a friend. Having said all that, the coaches didn't want anybody getting hurt. After Kyle, our 125 lbs boxer, took too many shots in the first round, Joe sent Mark over to their corner to ask them to ease up.

"Si, si."

Kyle lost the second and third rounds also, but his opponent pulled punches and backed up instead of going for a knockout.

The fourth fight was at 160 lbs. This was my natural weight, but Joe said no to me fighting any of their guys. Instead they put on an exhibition where two of their fighters, weighing 157 and 159, went at it. I had to admit, they were both clearly out of my class.

"Ready kid?" Mark asked me.

"Yeah." He held the ropes open and I stepped in.

Fighting at 165 I should have been a bit smaller than my opponent, but I wasn't.

I entered the ring around 158 lbs. I'm guessing he was the full 165 lbs, and about two inches shorter than me. I felt his power, pushing me around in the clinch a few times, and landing short body blows while we were tied up, but it was far less than sparring with Darrius.

I threw a few punches, my form noticeably falling apart every time I did. After two minutes of sub-par boxing from two first timers, the bell rang.

"Did I win that round?" I asked Joe as I sat on the stool.

"I tell you who lost is the crowd. Do you remember anything that I taught you?"

"Yeah, yeah, I'm trying."

"Just do what you do in the gym kid, use those fast hands. Punch move, punch again."

I have to admit, the first half of the second round was more of the same. We were sloppy. He pushed and clinched a lot. I was a bit gun shy and not firing punches when I should have been.

The second half of the second round went much better for me. Here was the difference. As we came together in another clinch, I heard him gasping for air. He was tired. I lost all fear, he didn't have the energy to come at my anymore, I knew that I could attack at will. I did.

For the next minute I let my hands go, landing fast and often.

On the stool again, Mark gave me some water.

"That's boxing!" Joe told me. "You understand now? Be the matador."

Their assistant coach came over and said something to Mark, who nodded and looked at Joe.

"Ok kid." Joe said again, "just the jab this round. Put a jab out there, slip, use your footwork, work your defense, move and jab again. Work to his body with both hands. Don't fire any more power shots to the head."

After my match I watched Luke easily take control of the first round of his 175 lbs fight.

While I was in the shower, I missed what I heard was a tremendous bout between Darrius and a really seasoned 185 lbs vet from their team. No matter how many times Joe talked about being the matador, Darrius just moved forward. He was willing to take punishment if it meant getting to land hard shots. Joe hated it. Crowds loved it.

I went back out into the gym in time to see the real fight.

At 6'4 and 225 lbs Stephan Bonnar entered the ring. Across from him stood a legitimate professional boxer, what is commonly referred to as a journeyman. A journeyman is a fighter who has been around for a long time. He's never going to crack the top ten, likely never going to get fights on TV, or be flown to Vegas, but he's dangerous. He has the skill to beat all but the best up and comers, but he is often used as nothing more than a body for the real prospects to beat on. Most journeyman have been fighting professionally for over ten years. Many no longer train, they work a manual labor job to make money and stay in some kind of shape, then they take a low paying professional fight every single week-end. Promoters use them to make their hometown boy look good, and to build up their records.

Stephan's opponent was Mexican, in his late 30s, maybe even early 40s, 5'11 and 235 lbs, with a professional boxing record of 17 wins and 42 defeats.

They wore 10 once gloves and no headgear. Scheduled for four three-minute rounds, this would be a real fight, nobody was going to ask the other corner to lighten up. Everyone in the gym crowded around.

Stephan started the fight off fast, landing hard shots to the head and gloves from the outside. His opponent was tough though, he worked inside and got to Stephan's body, landing half a dozen clean hard body shots in the first round.

In the second round Stephan poured it on. A clobbering right hand sent Stephan's opponent to the mat. He staggered to his knees as the referee counted. He was alert and ready to go by the count of six, but he stayed down until the referee said diez, ten. Knowing that he was outmatched, he opted not to take any more punishment tonight.

They say it takes a comic seven years to find his voice. I

don't know if that's exactly true, but I can tell you that it takes a long time. In all honesty I don't believe I ever completely found mine. I didn't stay in the business for a full seven years. I do know that the more I got on stage, I became more comfortable. Slowly I became more and more like me, and less like Jerry. For now though, I was basically a Seinfeld clone.

"Why are you doing Seinfeld's act?" A fellow comic asked me after a set.

"That's not Seinfeld's act."

"Yes it is."

"No, it's not."

"Yes it is."

"It's not, but this conversation doesn't seem to be going anywhere."

As I walked away, I heard him telling the table, "That guy's doing Seinfeld's act."

"Don't worry about him," Rylan said, "I've seen him, he's a complete no talent hack. He sucks."

He did have a point though. Nothing that I performed was Jerry's material, I wrote every word, but I smiled like Jerry, paused like Jerry, wrote like Jerry. Everything about my act was Jerry's voice. Slowly it would evolve into my own, but this took me a long time.

Rylan seemed to know his voice from the second he stepped on a stage. But he couldn't figure out how to control an audience. He'd go weeks making every audience he stepped in front of have tears in their eyes from laughing so hard, then a month without a chuckle.

Headliners, the solid journeymen comics who work the club circuit every weekend, the grinders who long ago gave up on the dream of comedic fame and fortune, they knew how to control a crowd.

I studied them.

They started off strong. The first five minutes they used tried and true material, never going off book, and they won the crowd. They told the crowd, "You like me. You're having fun. You want to laugh tonight." Then they coasted. For the next forty-five minutes they put out material that was just so-so, chatted with the front row, improvised a little, and did typical low-level jokes that they'd written years and years ago. The crowds loved it.

"This guy's a no talent hack." Rylan would say from the back. He wasn't entirely wrong. The low-level headliners weren't great talents, but they had worked their craft and understood how to put on a good show every night.

After coasting for most of the show on moderately funny, and fairly obvious, jokes, they would then end with their very strongest five minutes, leaving the crowd a memory of how funny they were.

They knew how to work a room. There was much to be learned from these journeymen comics.

"You get injured, it's your problem. Sign here." A bouncer handed me a clipboard with a piece of paper. I signed the waiver form, highly doubting if it would hold up in court, but not caring.

I was in the backroom of a huge bar, Joe's on Weed Street. The backroom had a ring set up, and about two hundred folding chairs around it. Darrius "The Welsh Windmill", and Luke came with me.

"Take off whatever you want, jump on the scale."

I stripped down to my boxer shorts and stepped onto a typical bathroom scale.

"One sixty-one" the bouncer said. "I got a guy who just came in, weighs one sixty-six, you want to fight him?"

"Sure."

"Ok, next."

Darrius, our gym's super-middleweight, stepped onto the scale. He fought his Golden Glove bouts at 168 lbs, but tonight, fighting at his natural walking around weight, he weighed 184.

"I'll fight any man 199 or under." He told the bouncer and the bouncer nodded.

"Next!"

Luke wrapped my hands. The backroom was full of drunks, waitresses in tiny outfits, and twenty or so fighters.

I say fighters 'cause most weren't really boxers. A few were, but most were local tough guys, or simply guys who thought they were tough.

In the ring, two heavyweights pushed each other around. They both outweighed Stephan, one by as much as a hundred pounds, but that was fat, it wasn't real weight. Even at over 300 lbs, I doubt if either could punch nearly as hard as Darrius.

Speaking of Darrius, he had won his fight in thirty-eight seconds of pure violence.

After watching him absolutly destroy a 195 lbs man I felt much better about how far I had come since my first day at Kahne's Korner.

"Do you go that hard when we're sparring?"

"No mate."

Ok, never mind.

I stepped into the ring, no headgear, eight-ounce gloves.

I had my boxing gear on, Luke had wrapped my hands. Across from me my opponent wore jeans, pulled off his t-shirt, and his buddy put his hands straight into the gloves.

"Be the matador." Luke told me.

The bell rang and he charged right at me, firing full steam with looping lefts and rights. I blocked everything, gloves up, rolling well. I slipped out a few times, landed a few jabs, but was again quickly pushed to the ropes under a barrage of punches. Before I knew it, the bell rang and our first round was over.

"You're doing alright." Luke told me. "Your defense is good, but you're not punching enough. Remember, roll two shots, three at the most, then counter. Right now, you're just rolling. I counted eleven in a row that you rolled without firing back. Two shots, then fire a counter, every time."

He gave me some water. The referee, who was just one of the club's bouncers, yelled "Seconds out!"

"He's going to tire." Luke said as he left the ring.

Again I was pushed against the ropes. For roughly thirty seconds I defended as I heard Darrius yelling "Get out of the fooking corner!"

Then I shoulder rolled a right hand and fired a straight right down the middle.

That was all it took, one punch to his wide-open chin and he fell backwards in the middle of the ring. The crowd cheered. It was the perfect set up, and the perfect punch line.

"You won't be ready yet."

"I'm ready."

I stood at the back of Zannie's Comedy Club, the most legit professional standup comedy club in Chicago, begging the manager/owner to give me a chance to perform. If I did well, this could be it, I could be turning pro.

"How long have you been doing comedy."

"I've done seventy-four sets now." A few of the professional comics at the back table chuckled. Only rookies count how many times they've been on stage. When you've lost count long ago, then you're beginning to understand comedy.

"Why don't you come back in a year?"

"I'm funny right now."

The manager looked at me. I didn't look funny.

I turned to the three professional comics sitting at the back table. One of them was Leonard, a thirty something black guy who I knew. I wouldn't say we were friends, but we were friendly. He was getting booked as an opener now, sometimes, and still hit the better open mics on any nights when he wasn't getting paid.

"He knows me."

The manager looked at Leonard. "Is he good?"

"He's doing it. He's getting some laughs."

"Is he ready?"

Leonard turned around and went back to his previous conversation.

"Just take a look at me man!" I said again.

The manger shrugged. "Five minutes, tight. Put him up between the opener and the feature." Then he turned and went back to the kitchen. I sat at the professional comic table. In retrospect I'm sure they all chuckled again as I took out my notes and rehearsed in my head.

The set went well. I got some laughs.

"So?" I asked the manager excitedly at the back of the room while he stood and watched the feature.

"It wasn't bad. You got promise. Keep working it."

"What about here? How about some dates to work as an opener?

"You're not ready."

After six months of training, and a 2-0 record, I entered a tournament.

"Just relax." Mark talked to me as he wrapped my hands. "It's a sixteen-man tournament, so the most you'll fight over the weekend is four times. But there's no pressure. How's that feel?"

I flexed my left hand. The wraps felt great. "Good."

"Joe doesn't expect you to come away from this thing the champion, we just want to get you some experience in a real match. Now what are you going to do?"

"Circle right, keep him at the end of my jab."

"That's right."

At 5'10 I was one of the taller fighters in the 147 lbs class. I would have the reach advantage. Joe had taught me over the last six months to stay on the outside, and to circle right, away from a right-handed opponent's power hand.

Mark finished wrapping my hands. "Ok, just hang out and stay loose. Win, lose, or draw, you're going to do something great today kid."

I walked around. I had weighed in at 148, within the one-pound margin of error that they allow for the 147 class. Now, after a plate of food and a few bottles of water, I was back in the high 150s. The other guys in the 147 class all weighed 155 to 160 as well. They were all black or Mexican. They all eyed me with hate.

"Hey." I looked to my left. A guy in his mid-20s sat in the bleachers, shoes laced up, hands wrapped, towel over his head. A white guy. "You 147?"

"Yeah."

He motioned for me to join him, and I did.

"Gino."

"Joel."

"How many fights you got?"

"Two, both wins. You?"

"Seven and two. Don't let them get to you." He waved his hand at the other fourteen guys fighting at 147.

"I'm not."

"They'll all stare at you, try to act like tough guys. Doesn't mean shit. All that South Chicago bullshit, they can't bring it into the ring with them. I've whipped three of them already. Maybe four. I don't know, they all look the same, you know what I mean?"

I didn't answer.

"So what are you?"

"Huh?"

"I'm guessing Jewish. But not like the American pussy Jews, more like those mean bastards over in Israel."

"Jewish Irish mix."

He nodded. "Gino. I'm Italian." He stuck out his hand, so I shook it. "Lot of short guys here. Just work your jab, keep them on the outside, hopefully we don't meet till the finals."

I nodded.

"Hang on, they're doing the draw."

A giant white board sat empty, the numbers one through sixteen on it. A man drew a name out of a bowl.

"The first fighter will be…"

He read Gino's name. "That's me." Gino told me.

"And his first-round opponent is…" The man opened the piece of paper. "From Kahne's Korner, Joel Paul Rez, Resilick, Rise…"

I had made one ally, and now we were matched up in the

first round.

I circled right. Gino, a left-handed fighter, smashed me with a straight left. I jabbed. Gino, at around six foot one, easily stepped out of range. This pattern continued throughout the first round.

"What the hell do I do?" I yelled at Joe as Mark gave me some water.

"Circle the other way."

"What?!"

"He's left-handed. Everything is opposite. And you have to work inside, he's taller than you are."

"I don't know how to work inside!"

"Every punch a left hander throws, all your defense is opposite. And you have to duck, the rolling and stepping back won't work against a taller opponent."

"You haven't taught me how to do any of that shit!"

"You want me to call it off?"

"No."

"Well, you got one round to figure it out!"

The bell rang. Mark took the stool away, the ref told us to fight. Everything that I had been taught was preparing me for the most likely fighter, a right hander who was an inch or two shorter than I am. Gino was left-handed and tall.

I tried rushing in wildly, but this was Gino's tenth fight. He jabbed, circled, moved, jabbed again, moved, and stung me with straight left power shots every time I stepped the wrong way.

Halfway through the second round, the ref stopped the contest and raised Gino's hand.

I studied at Second City, Improv Olympic, and Go Comedy. I took a class from, and became real friends with, Chris Stole who would later be in every episode of Chicago Fire. I did over a hundred short films as an actor. Most of them were terrible, but I was learning by doing. I got into a movie with a very small role. Also, with an equally small role, was a guy named Paul Walter Hauser, who would later star as the title character in Clint Eastwood's Richard Jewell. I hung out, and performed on an improv team, with Tim Baltz who is now a regular cast member on an HBO show.

In the early evenings I was at the boxing gym. Joe taught me the shoulder roll, slipping and punching to the body, and proper angles to set my attack while simultaneously keeping me safe. We also started talking about taller fighters and left-handed fighters!

Then, in the evenings, Rylan and I would hit the open mics, working my standup while getting me, on average, an extra workout of roughly ten miles of bike riding per night just riding from club to club.

I trained more. I did more standup. My record grew to 4 – 1. My comedy became sharper and sharper, laughs coming more predictably and more often.

Every night, often at three am, I studied. I watched thirty minutes of Jerry Seinfeld, followed by thirty minutes of Floyd Mayweather. I moved like them, I thought like them, and every time I stepped in front of a crowd, I became one of them.

For money, I had a day job. Being the odd sort that I am, I somehow landed the least city job possible, while living in America's second largest city.

I drove a horse and carriage around downtown for The Royal Horse carriage company (name slightly changed for legal purposes).

I'd been around horses most of my life, during the summers anyway, and enjoyed working in barns. I'd never driven a carriage before, but within a few hours I had the hang of it, and a week later the City of Chicago issued me a carriage driver's license.

My manager was a guy named Don, a fifty-year-old know it all in a bad tuxedo. He started out alright, teaching me how to tack up, talking too much but pleasantly, and blabbering on and on about who I couldn't trust in the barn. Apparently, it was everybody.

The next day he wore the same cheap tuxedo. He wore it every day. Imagine what that tuxedo looks like when you work around horses all day and do your wash once a month. An old English top hat made him appear to be almost average height, while simultaneously covering his thin comb over. He looked like Danny DeVito as The Penguin.

On an average eight-hour day we stayed pretty busy, giving about ten rides of thirty minutes each. At $25 per ride we would go home at night with $250 dollars in our pocket for the company, in the other pocket would be our tips. Tips averaged about $10 per ride, so generally we'd make a hundred dollars, plus the minimum wage check that we'd receive every other week.

Every day I'd tack up a horse, hook him to a carriage, then drive straight through the Cabrini-Green housing project on my way to downtown. At night, with between $200 and $500 in cash in my pocket, I again drove a horse and carriage back through the same projects, hoofs clapping on the pavement, in the dark.

Cabrini-Green was a government housing project on the North side of Chicago. At its peak it was home to 15,000 low/no income people living in a total of 3,600 units.

By the time I was there, roughly half the units were torn down, the other half still in use. Of course, the rubble of torn down units was still used as homes, urinals, brothels, drug dens, and gang headquarters. Cabrini-Green had crime of every sort.

People think of the South as racist and the North as integrated. If anything, the opposite is true. People live side by side in the South. Chicago is a segregated city. Cabrini-Green started decades ago as a low/no income project for Italians. In time, they all moved out. Now, as I drove a horse and carriage through it, it was entirely black.

It was a very dangerous neighborhood. Especially at night. Especially when you're a white boy, driving a horse and carriage, and returning from a shift with hundreds of dollars of cash stuffed in your pockets.

"Don't worry." Don told me. "These people are all afraid of horses."

At the end of every shift Don demanded a $20 dollar "commission", per driver, per night. It was his tax for getting us the job and allowing us to keep it.

Many of the drivers were fresh off the boat Poles, they didn't have any choice. They'd be at work for ten to twelve hours, cleaning out stalls, grooming horses, and driving their horse from the stables to the downtown water tower area where we set up every day. Pay didn't start until the horse arrived downtown. Pay ended when the horse left downtown. Work generally ended about two hours later.

Sure, the workers got screwed. But they had it better than the horses. Chicago law protected the horses, they could only be on the street for one eight-hour shift per day. It's a good law, in theory. A hundred-dollar bill was passed every day from Don to the local police officer who walked by on his beat, and the horses stayed out for sixteen hours a day.

One day Don came into the barn in a practically foul mood. Yelling at everybody, as he often did, he looked at my friend Yuri who had spent the last hour getting his horse ready and was about to leave. Don unhooked the buckles from his horse and threw all of his tack on the ground.

"Start over and do it how I told you this time!"

Yuri was a great guy. About a decade older than me, in his mid-thirties, he had come to America recently along with his wife and young son. Now his wife was pregnant again.

He was a friendly guy and a hard worker. But his English was limited and I doubt if he had the equivalent of a high school degree back in Poland. His options were few.

Like a beat dog, Yuri gathered up the gear to start his morning over.

Don barked something at me. I mumbled "whatever" and turned my back on him.

He didn't like this. He didn't like being slighted. He was not the owner, but in every way, he considered this to be his barn.

I felt him grab me and ram me into the wall. He wasn't in

shape, he wasn't an athlete, but he was 200 lbs and we hit the wall hard.

He kept me pinned there for a minute, his right-hand clawing at my face. I closed my eyes tightly as he tried to shove his thumb into my eye.

I pushed his hand off and managed to spin. Still pinned to the wall we fought for a few more seconds, then I was able to create space.

Don came rushing back at me, running directly into my left jab. His nose broke. My right hand to his chin followed, and he dropped like a bag of coal at my feet.

Joe was right, I had very fast hands back then.

"Don, you alright?" I looked down at him. It was my first reaction, far too nice of me really. This bum had tried to put out my eye. By all rights I should have stomped on his head while he lay unconscious.

"He alright." Leon, a black driver looked at him. "Nose broke. Jaw might be broke. But he snoring away like a baby, racist old son of a bitch." Then Leon grinned, "Yuri, give me a hand here."

Yuri and Leon picked Don up and dragged him, still snoring, across the barn. Then they threw him, face down, into the giant pile of horse shit.

"Hey kid!" Joe called across the gym to me. "You ready to get that loss off your record?"

Getting a loss off your record meant rematch. The original loss would never come off of your record of course, but if you could best the man who bested you, it would erase the loss in your mind. For me, the rematch could only be against one guy; Gino.

"Yeah, of course."

"Promoter friend of mine is putting on a smoker in three weeks. Gino's already said yes to the bout, it's yours if you want it."

"Of course I want it."

"Get in the ring, let's teach you how to fight a tall southpaw."

A southpaw was a left-handed fighter. Used pretty much

only in boxing now, it was originally a baseball term. The American Heritage Dictionary of the English Language tells us that the word southpaw originated from the practice in baseball of arranging the diamond with the batter facing east to avoid the afternoon sun. This would mean that a normal right-handed pitcher's body would face the North when he threw, but a left hander, the ball in his left paw, would have to face the South.

For the next three weeks I worked daily, training twice as hard as normal. I learned to go under a taller fighter's straight punches and hit his body, I learned to move in the opposite direction against a left hander, and I learned to fire my right hand first and my left second.

Luke was able to fight both orthodox and southpaw. He switched to only southpaw for me, letting me spar with him every time he was in the gym. Luke was taller than me, slick, sparring as a southpaw, and a bit stronger than Gino. It was excellent work for me.

A smoker was a different kind of boxing match. It was a private event, sometimes a charity, sometimes a stag party at a rich club, often at an Elks Lodge, VA, or other fraternal organization. There would be boxing, ring girls in bikinis (even topless), and cigars passed out to the crowd. Smoke filled the air and wafted between you and your opponent. Headgear wasn't worn, knockouts were highly encouraged.

Gino entered the ring first. At six foot one he was exceptionally tall for 147 lbs. You would think he'd be incredibly skinny, but he really wasn't. He'd later tell me that he walked around at 165, the weight that most 154 lbs fighters walk around at, a full seven pounds more than me. He entered on his own, his older Italian trainer not with him tonight, just one assistant coach to give him water. He looked in shape.

Joe and Mark lead me in next. The crowd cheered. They really wanted to get to the heavier weight classes, the ones that produced the most likely knock outs, but they were game to watch any good scrape.

Mark held open the ropes and I stepped in. Gino walked across the ring and held out his glove.

"Hey, how are ya? How ya been?"

"Yeah, I'm ok. You?"

"Not my best day, but what are you going to do? Come out hard man, let's give them a good show."

We touched gloves again and he walked back to his corner.

The ref asked if both corners were ready and a bell rang.

There were no jabs, no feeling out process. Gino wanted to see if he could stop me in the first round. He came forward hard, firing away. I ducked and pounded to the body. He held me and fired shots to my kidneys and the back of my head.

Joe stood on the ring, complaining to the referee. But this was not a sanctioned fight. It was a smoker, a street fight with gloves on, for the entertainment of a mob. The referee was not even a real ref, he was just some guy from the club who was somewhat athletic and had seen a few boxing matches.

Again and again we came together. I counted the number of times I landed cleanly to the body. Seven, eight… My goal was to land ten hard body blows in the first round, to really slow him down.

Gino pushed, grabbed, punched on the break, and hit me hard with an elbow right when the bell rang.

Mark set my stool. Joe entered the center of the ring, yelling at the referee. Seconds later he knelt in front of me.

"Your eye ok?"

"Yeah, his elbow caught my forehead. I win that round?"

"Maybe, it was close. Who the hell knows at these things? The judges are drunk and don't know a damned thing about boxing!"

Round two started. We fired hard shots in the center of the ring. I continued to work the body, but this time mixed it up to the head too.

The ref broke us. Gino came forward hard with a right jab. I slipped it to the outside and fired a straight right up the middle. It caught him flush as he was coming forward.

He fell. A clean knockout.

My phone rang. I didn't recognize the number, but it was from the Chicago 312 area code. I picked up.

"Hello?"

"Joel?"

"Yeah."

"It's Gino."

"Who?"

"Gino. We fought a couple of times. You knocked me out at the Elk's Lodge a few nights ago."

I looked at my phone. I don't know why people do this, stare at an inanimate object as if it will give them more information, somehow explain to me what the hell was going on.

After a brief pause Gino spoke again. "I called over to the gym, your coach gave me your number."

I paused again, absurdly looking again to my phone for an explanation. It did not offer me one, so I just spoke.

"Hey man. What's up?"

"I'm at a bar downtown. You want to meet me?"

"What kind of beer do you drink?"

"I normally don't."

"Well if you did?"

"I'll take a Guinness."

Gino motioned to the bartender. "Alex, get my friend a Guinness, my tab."

"You don't have to do that."

"I came at you too aggressively."

"I learned how to move against a left-handed fighter."

"Yeah, you did. Where are you from? And don't tell me Chicago. I'm sick of you rich boys saying you're from Chicago when you're actually from Wilmette or some other North suburb."

"Michigan."

"Michigan. College guy?"

"Yeah."

"Rich?"

"I'm not."

"But your dad is."

"He does alright."

"That means rich."

"It means what it means."

"It means he don't work in a meat packing plant like my old man."

"He's a criminal defense attorney."

"Yeah that's about what I thought." Gino took a shot, then a sip of his beer. "I like you, I don't know why, I just do. I knew right away, first time that we talked. Knew you were rich too. Don't matter. You are who you are, you know? Can't help it. Where you're from, how you grew up, none of that shit matters. People wonder why a rich kid would fight, but I don't. Doesn't matter where you were born, if you're a fighter, you have to fight."

"I moved to Chicago to be a standup comedian."

Gino looked at me. "Shut the hell up."

"It's true. I wanted to train at Second City."

"You're funny?"

"Some people think so. I'm doing standup now, almost every night."

"Well shit. I'll get a couple of girls and we'll come see you. What kind of girls do you like?"

"Good looking ones."

"I like the kind that say yes." Then he yelled at the bartender, "Hey Alex! You remember when I slept with your sister in High School? My friend here needs her number and another Guinness!"

"We'll take a bowl of those pretzels too please. As long as we're ordering food and disrespecting your sister. Thank you."

"His sister slept with half the neighborhood, ain't my fault."

Alex brought a bowl of pretzels and another beer. I noticed that he did not include his sister's phone number. "How do you know this guy?", he motioned at Gino.

"He knocked me out a couple of nights ago."

Alex looked at Gino, then back at me. "Yeah?" Then he looked me up and down again. Seeing beyond the suburban front this time and noticing intense eyes and tight muscles hidden under my clothes.

"Knocked me out cold."

"Well, I'm glad somebody did. This one's on the house guy."

Alex walked away.

"You can't help it, can you?" Gino asked me.

"What's that?"

"Fighting."

"I don't get into many street fights. Had one here at work just a bit ago, but I couldn't help it."

"That's for bums. Throw a punch, push a guy, cowards do that 'cause they know it's all going to get broken up in under thirty seconds. You and me, we walk into a ring, feed off of a crowd watching us. You know you're going to fight for weeks ahead of time and you still go through with it. That's real. What's it called when you kill someone, and you plan it?"

"Pre-meditated."

"That's it. That's us, we're pre-meditated murderers. The real deal. You can't help that shit man. People think that coming from a certain place makes you tough, but that ain't it, you're either born cursed as a fighter, or you're not."

He downed the last few swallows of his beer and ordered another. "You want to know something?"

"Yeah, sure."

"My father died. A few days before our fight."

"I'm sorry."

Gino shrugged. "I think when you share the ring with somebody multiple times you form a bond with them, whether you want to or not. You know what I'm saying?"

I did. Gino was the only guy who I had fought twice, and both fights were brutal. Both ended in a KO.

"Look," he went on, "I'm not saying we're friends. And I'm not saying we're not either, I'm just saying that life tied you and me together. It just is what it is."

Six of my teammates hung out at a sports bar in Old Town for UFC fight night. Gino and I came in about twenty minutes after the event had started and joined them.

Since our night at the bar we had begun training together during the days, three times a week. We would meet down by the lake. Sometimes we'd do long bike rides down to the museum district and back, but mostly we ran sprints on the beach, did endless pushups, pullups on play structures, leg raises, sit ups, and flexed while one guy put on a glove and punched the other twenty times in the stomach, then switched.

He continued to train technique at his gym, and I stayed at mine, but these meetings really upped both of our strength and conditioning.

Unlike our first night out together, we both cut out the beer. We didn't talk much, but there was no question that we were friends now. I was also dating, if you could call it that, his cousin Isabelle, who was also his girlfriend's best friend.

Most of my nights were still consumed by training, followed by standup comedy, but free nights were spent with Gino and our girls. Often the three of them would come to my shows.

The guys from my gym quickly accepted him as a part of our group.

"What did we miss?" Gino asked and pointed to one of the big screen TVs.

"First prelim. Ref stopped the contest in the second round. Shonie won't be up for two more fights."

Shonie Carter was something of a local legend in the Chicago fight world. A middle weight, a welterweight, a light heavy weight, Shonie would fight you. He taught classes here and there and stopped into all the Chicago gyms to train from time to time. He was a local judo champion, Illinois karate champion, a junior college wrestling champion, a kickboxer, a boxer, and a bouncer at a Mexican restaurant.

He was also just a character. He enjoyed dressing the part of the pimp, flashy colorful suits, canes, top hats, scarfs, and big sunglasses. I believe I met him roughly six times during my years in Chicago. He was always cool to me, but he introduced himself every single time like he had never seen me before in his life.

Signed by the UFC, he was never a serious contender for a world championship, but he was a good fighter. Now, years after the events of this story took place, the internet has his cage fighting record at 51 wins and 32 loses. They also list a kickboxing record of 57 and 5. Another site claims that he had over 250 total fights. I doubt if anyone, including Shonie, really knows.

Some see UFC, cage fighting, as violent, and of course it is. But violent sports have always been around. Pick an era, pick a culture, you'll find violence.

American slaves used to keep themselves entertained with sporting events called Battle Royals. The contests were essentially boxing matches, generally bare knuckle, with multiple men fighting in the ring at a time. The fights would continue until only one man remained. It is mistakenly thought that masters forced their slaves to fight, but this is largely untrue. The slaves were far too valuable for a master to wish to risk his property.

We assume that these barbaric events are far in our rearview mirror, and maybe many of them are, but the truth is that the injury rates in modern hockey and American football are off the charts. Violence is always going to be a part of the human experience; it's better to just accept that, bottle it up, and regulate it.

As we watched the fights a guy walked by our table. He was about 5'8, bald, goatee, and puffed out from too many steroid assisted hours at the gym. His arms, shoulders, and neck were huge. His t-shirt was the smallest size that he could squeeze in to.

At 6'4 Stephan Bonner towered over the crowd. He weighed about 225 lbs, but he was a true 225 lbs. There are very few men who are meant to weigh over 200 lbs. Most of us are built to be in the 140 to 170 range.

The average weight of a freshly recruited solider in WW2 was 144 lbs. They were a lot smaller, fitter, and they had guts. The kind of guts you need to fight a war, not the beer guts that guys walk around with now. The average WW2 solider carried a 64-pound pack, a ten-pound rifle, and could hike four miles, in full gear, in under an hour. Good luck to any pumped-up meat head who wanted to try to match that.

The spark plug with the goatee walked by our table, then, in typical High School bully fashion, he bumped his shoulder into Stephan.

Stephan grinned, then went back to watching the TV.

"You got a problem?"

We all looked at the guy. He looked like he could pick a car up straight over his head and throw it, but that wouldn't help him here.

"No." Stephan smiled again and went back to watching the TV.

"What are you, some kind of pussy?"

"I just want to watch Shonie fight man. Don't do something you're going to regret."

"Like what? Kick your ass?"

Darrius looked at him. "You're talking to the wrong table mate."

"Oh, bunch of tough guys huh? What's the matter with you then, you have to have the little Irish guy talk for you?"

"I'm Welsh ya bastard, an I'll do ya fookin' head in."

Stephan put his hand on Darrius' chest, stopping him. Then he looked back at the muscle shark. "Dude, I promise you, there's a much easier fight for you around the corner. Go away."

The walking muscle moved away, and we went back to the TV. I went to eating!

Most nights I took both my training and my diet seriously. But I also watched my wallet. This bar had three-dollar hamburgers and all you can eat baskets of fries for the tables. Too good to pass up!

I dug into my hamburger while simultaneously stuffing fries into my mouth.

Soon, Shonie Carter made his way to the cage and the entire Chicago bar erupted. He wasn't from our gym, but he was from our city. He came by the gym about once a month or so, picking up some tips from Joe, sparring with Darrius, then training with Carlson Gracie Sr. He trained this way at all the Chicago gyms.

As he made his way to the ring, it was clear that Shonie was drunk. He wore a crown, a purple cape, and carried a golden goblet. He danced, drank, and spilled wine.

In the ring the fight was tight, until Shonie spun around and struck his opponent with a backfist, the Shonie Carter Pimp Slap as he calls it, and knocked him out. The crowd went nuts. Shonie, in his purple speedo, danced in the middle of the cage.

After the fights we all poured out of the bar.

Directly behind us was the muscle head in the tight t-shirt, and his buddies.

"Hey!"

We turned. Stephan saw him and laughed. "Dude, go home."

Stephan turned his back, the muscle head shoved him. It was a poor choice.

Stephan spun and cracked him with an uppercut. The sound was horrific. Blood gushed, teeth flew, a body dropped to the sidewalk.

The evening ended with the six of us waiting in a hospital lobby while a doctor had to surgically remove one of the muscle head's teeth from Stephan's right knuckles.

Over the next six months I developed, both as a boxer, a comedian, and a friend to Gino.

I fought as often as a I could, at least once a month, at Joe's on Weed Street. The fights were different than in the gym, they were wild, almost like street fights. I learned to bob and weave under haymakers, to counter off of an opponent throwing bombs, to stick and move from the outside.

I pictured myself exactly like Floyd Mayweather, and in time I was able to move exactly like him. Being on the ropes didn't bother me at all, I was perfectly comfortable pinned against the ropes with my opponent firing away. Just like Floyd, I rolled my shoulder away from the right-hand bombs, then pivoted the opposite way and let a looping left hand harmlessly roll into my right glove.

While being shelled on the ropes I was able to interact with the crowd if I wanted to, dropping in a quick "how you doing?" or smiling to girls in the front rows. Then, whenever I was ready, I could counter and land cleanly to my opponents over exposed chin, or duck a bomb and step back to the middle of the ring to continue working my jab.

On those same nights I would bike over to an open mic comedy room, meet up with Rylan, and take to the stage to work my new material.

I'd see Gino and our girlfriends at least once a week. He went to my fights, I went to his, he came with the girls to my shows.

The truth is, I relied 100% on Gino to pick us up girls. I just showed up, performed, either as a fighter or a comedian, and hoped the girls he brought were impressed. They were all from his neighborhood, Italian or Polish, high school educated if we were lucky. At 26 Gino didn't know anybody who didn't work in the meat packing plant, and he hardly knew a girl over 19 who didn't have a kid.

I was dating his cousin, but one night he showed up with two new girls.

"Where's Mary and Isabelle?"

"Yeah, we broke up with them. This is Becky."

"Alright."

Dating for us was a far different world than the crowd who populated the North side of Chicago. That was a five hundred dollar a night crowd, blowing money on shows, dinners, expensive bars, and taxis to take them from one stop to another.

We rode the eL, the elevated train, Chicago's metro. Most of the places we went were free to us – either Gino or I were fighting, or I was performing. We walked our dates through the back doors, bouncers not bothering or caring that they were under 21, made our way through the kitchen saying hello to the Mexican staffs that we grew to know, and found a table in the back.

Gino and I were in training, no alcohol for us. These girls had never heard of any beers that weren't Bud Light, and the waitresses all gave me their employee discounts.

It was a dating budget that I could afford, even if just barely.

During this time my standup routines drew constant laughs, my boxing record swelled to 11 – 1, and I had the ego from both to match.

Dana White, president of the UFC, announced a new show, The Ultimate Fighter, better known as TUF. It was a reality show with sixteen unsigned fighters living in a Vegas mansion together. At the end of every week, there was a fight to see who gets to stay in the house. The winner of the tournament got a UFC contract.

The entire bar tuned in to see Stephan Bonner on the TV every week!

Myself, Gino, Darrius, Luke, and a few other guys from the gym ate three-dollar hamburgers and bragged to the room that we trained with Stephan. He was the Heavyweight Champion of Chicago, and he was from our gym!

The show was the typical reality show nonsense, if I'm being honest. Someone was making too much noise and keeping the entire house awake, someone else threw another contestant's suitcase in the pool, Stephan literally got into an argument with another fighter because he didn't like the way that Diego Sanchez ate broccoli.

But at the end of each episode there was a fight. Tonight, the entire bar erupted when Stephan defeated Mike "Quick" Swick with two seconds left in the first round!

Our table cheered the loudest. When our gym's champion won, it felt like we had done something great ourselves.

"160 pounds! Have you lost your mind?"

Joe was looking at the lineup for an upcoming show. Four of my teammates had signed up with me, all using common sense and following Joe's instructions. I had decided that I was done cutting weight. I hated the routine of not taking even a sip of water all day, jumping rope with three layers of sweats on, sitting in the sauna till I felt like I was going to die – all so I could weigh in at 147 lbs, then drink and eat just to return to 159 lbs a day later for the fight.

I was done with it. I weighed 160 lbs, why shouldn't I just fight at 160 lbs?

My opponent wasn't better than me, but neither was he worse. I had fought guys at Joe's on Weed Street who weighed in as high as 179 lbs, but they were untrained. They had normal athletic builds, not the hard-compact muscle of a fighter. They were what we called cans, bums, roobs, drunks.

After one round of boxing, and being put on my ass twice, I realized that my opponent was not a bum. He was six feet tall, entered the ring completely ripped and close to a 180 lbs, and knew how to box.

I staggered my way back to my corner. Mark put out the stool, Joe kneeled in front of me.

"Well what do you say kid? You had enough?"

"I can do it Joe!"

The referee made his way to our corner. "How's he doing coach?"

"We're done."

The ref nodded. "Good." He walked to the center of the ring and waved his arms.

"Joe, I can do it!" Mark was taking off my headgear.

Joe shook his head, "Come on kid, we're going home."

A few weeks later I got to step into a boxing ring, and use my standup comedy skills at the same time.

Our gym was holding a promo night. Downstairs two personal trainers put a couple of professional models through workouts as rich people wandered around with plastic glasses of champagne.

Soon they were ushered upstairs, where two of Mr. Gracie's top students put on a Brazilian Jujitsu demonstration.

Then the lights went on in our ring, and the crowd of a hundred or so gathered around. Darrius stood in one corner, Luke in the other, and I, as Joe's chosen ring announcer, had center stage.

"In the blue corner, weighing 172 lbs, this pretty-boy has

broken up with thirty-seven women and been dumped only once...” The crowd laughed, Luke laughed, I went on and made a few more jokes until Luke heard his name and raised his hands.

“And in the red corner, coming all the way from Wales, he weighed in at a confusing fourteen stone eight...”

On a Saturday night I scored a set at a decent room in Wrigleyville. It wasn’t a professional show, but there would only be eight comics on that night, getting a full fifteen minutes each. The club was selective, only the best amateurs, and many guys who were part time pros, got spots there.

Gino arrived and took a table in the back. He had his old girlfriend, and his cousin with him. I guess we were dating them again now. Fine.

Rylan had scored a set on the same night. I called him over to the table and introduced him to Gino.

“Gino!” Rylan popped his collar and danced around a bit like Saturday night fever. “Hey, hey, Gino!”

“That’s funny.” Gino grinned in a slightly amused and slightly annoyed way. “He’s a funny guy.”

I got my free iced tea, and even though Gino wasn’t a comic the waitress knew me and brought him a free Coke. The girls both ordered Bud Light, which with the waitress’ employee discount only cost Gino and me two dollars each.

Rylan made a crack about Gino spending all of this week’s spaghetti money, which brought another small, but not so happy, smile to Gino’s face.

I was up first. Gino and the girls wished me well, I took a sip of tea, and away I went.

I had a solid fifteen-minute set, the longest I’d ever done. I used tried and true material, didn’t take any real risks, and brought the crowd along for a fun ride with me. It wasn’t spectacular, but it was solid.

Rylan’s set that night was spectacular. I couldn’t begin to reproduce for you what he just organically did, but it was a hundred percent new material, and it was one hundred percent at Gino’s expense.

He danced around on stage like a character from the movie Greece, he talked like Rocky Balboa, he popped his collar and hit on girls in the crowd. It was hysterical.

The crowed loved it! The two girls at our table choked on laughter! Gino smiled a little, nodded his head from time to time, and silently fumed.

The five of us left the club and walked towards the eL. Rylan, in good cheer from having another excellent set, whistled as he walked, his untied shoelaces flopping all over the place.

We cut into an alley, as you do when you're walking in Chicago and know all of the shortcuts. As soon as we did, Gino spun. His right hand lashed out and grabbed Rylan by the balls, pushing him backwards against the brick wall, as his left hand locked around Brian's throat.

"You want to disrespect me! Huh! In front of my girlfriend! In front of my cousin!"

The girls were yelling. They swatted and slapped at Gino, which had about as much effect as shooting a bear with a bb gun.

I got into the middle and pushed Gino back, separating them.

"Get off of me!" Gino shoved me. He came forward, in his southpaw stance.

I kept my hands open, trying to calm him down, but I raised them near my head and put my right foot behind me.

"Gino stop!" One of the girls yelled.

Behind me Rylan popped his collar and laughed "Hey, I'm Gino. Welcome to 1972, I'm Gino! Oh!" He danced around like the 70s, laughing.

"I'll kill you!"

"Alright, say hi to Mario and Luigi for me." Rylan laughed as he moseyed away down the alley.

More time passed. I continued to fight. I continued to do standup. And, believe it or not, I kept my job as a carriage driver.

Evidently Don woke up in the giant pile of horse shit like it was just another Tuesday, and for him, maybe it was. Yuri told me that this was not his first altercation in the barn. He likely didn't want the owner to hear about it, so he never said another word about it to me. I came in, tacked up a horse like normal two or three days a week, and drove him down to the Water Tower Plaza to pick up rides all day.

The big news in my circle was the upcoming fight.

The main season of TUF had ended, and the final fighters had been sent back to their home gyms to train. For two hours a night Joe worked on Stephan's boxing. Then Calson Gracie took him for two more hours of Brazilian Juitisu. In the mornings, before practice, Stephan was downstairs lifting weights and working on his cardio.

Tonight was the fight. Stephan Bonnar vs Forrest Griffin for the TUF Season One championship and a UFC contract.

The bar was standing room only. Gino, Luke, Darrius, and ten other guys from our gym crowded around one tiny table, the only space we could find, and waited for the main event to come on.

Then the lights dimmed, music started, and there was Joe Kahne and Carlson Gracie, leading Stephan to a UFC cage.

The noise inside this bar was Chicago Cubs made the playoffs level!

Mark, Joe's assistant coach, was in particularly good cheer. He bought round after round for all the guys, getting everyone drunk on money he didn't have, running up a credit card bill like there was no tomorrow.

The fight started and they went to war! From the second the bell rung to the moment the third round ended Stephan and Forrest went forward in what is still widely considered one of, if not the, greatest fights in UFC history.

Joe Rogan called it "the Hagler-Hearns of UFC".

Dana White has called it "The most important fight in UFC history." At a time when UFC was in financial trouble, and perhaps fading into ruin, Stephan Bonnar and Forrest Griffin saved the company.

The bar was quiet as the ring announcer entered. In a two to one split decision, Forrest Griffin had defeated Stephan Bonnar.

We were all quiet, defeated ourselves, and yet we all knew that we had just seen both men do something truly remarkable.

Dana White entered the cage. He congratulated Forrest. Then we all cheered loudly when he said that he was going to award two contracts tonight, and gave Stephan his ticket to the big leagues as well.

On Monday evening every member of the gym showed up early! Sure we were there for training, but really we came to celebrate!

Never mind the fact that it was Stephan and not us who was in the greatest fight in UFC history, we all felt like we won! Stephan had a UFC contract! It was like we all had made it to the majors!

We piled into the gym laughing and giving each other high fives.

Joe sat on the side of the ring. He was back from Vegas. He didn't share any of our cheer.

"Circle up guys, quiet down."

He wasn't yelling, he wasn't angry, he looked sad and spoke in a whisper. "Joe, what's going on?"

"Mark is gone."

"Gone?"

"He's been battling demons for a long time. You all know that. Last night he… well."

"Joe?"

"He stepped in front of a train. Mark's gone boys."

A year after my first audition at Zannie's, I scored another. They brought in three unsigned comics for a packed Saturday night show, and gave us ten minutes each in front of the headliner.

"Hey look." Rylan said too loudly as the first of the three was on stage. "Zannie's hired a seal."

The club owner, who was also sitting in the back, looked at

him and said "shhh!"

"Oh my god, this isn't comedy, this guy's a hack, all jugglers are hacks, this sucks." Rylan slid down in his chair, head flopped backwards, arms dangling everywhere.

I agreed with Rylan. I think there's a place for jugglers, and other acts, but comedy clubs were not that place. True standup comedy was a battle that you entered every night. It was standing on stage naked, with nothing between you and the audience but a microphone, and taming them. It was a man's sport. Jugglers, ventriloquists, and all the others – they brought weapons to a fist fight. Afraid to look the audience in the eye and take them on head-to-head.

But there was not a place for jugglers. Vaudeville clubs had died out a long time ago.

A typical vaudeville performance was made up of a series of separate, unrelated, acts grouped together on a common bill. Types of acts have included popular and classical musicians, singers, dancers, comedians, trained animals, magicians, ventriloquists, strongmen, acrobats, clowns, illustrated songs, jugglers, one-act plays or scenes from plays, athletes, lecturing celebrities (that's celebrities giving a lecture by the way, not standing on stage being lectured to by an athlete), and literally any other act you can dream up!

The advent of moving pictures cut into vaudeville's revenue. Soon more and more theater houses were showing movies, and avoiding having to pay live performers. Vaudeville still lived in the upscale theaters, until the great depression more or less wiped it out.

Now they made their way onto our stages, unwelcome guests of the true comedians. As Rylan said "Zannie's had hired a seal."

The juggler exited and I was up next. I brought my tightest ten-minute act. I stared into the wall of light but talked to the crowd like I could see them perfectly. I felt their laughs, paused to let them, then hit them again just before they were fully done exhaling. The ten-minute round ended, and I knew I had won the fight.

Once again, I sat in the back of the room, at the comic's table. Another comic nodded at me. The headliner said "nice set kid."

"Thank you."

"I ain't talking about you." He pointed at the tits of a women sitting at the table next to me and walked away.

The MC brought Rylan onto the stage. He had been tearing it up these last few months. I was getting better, but he was phenomenal. Every set seemed different; the guy couldn't help but be hilarious. Everything that fell out of his mouth was funny, and everyone knew it. When Rylan was up, all the comics who were waiting outside would come to the back of the room to watch.

The club manager sat at my table. "You're ready."

"Yeah?!"

"Yeah. Let's get you booked to open here four times this year, and I'll get you on the phone with Carol, she books a lot of one nighters and small clubs across the Midwest."

I had done it. I was about to start my journey as a professional comedian.

Meanwhile, on stage, Rylan was in the middle of one of the worst bombs I have ever seen. He finally yelled an obscenity at the crowd, literally dropped his mic, and walked off of the stage. He continued yelling as he pushed by the bouncers and stormed out the front door.

The headliner turned to the club owner, legitimately upset, "This is what you set me up to follow?"

"Andrew, I'm sorry..."

The MC ran to the stage and tried to save the show, doing five more minutes of standard warm up material to somewhat get the crowd back before the headliner had to go on stage.

After going 17 wins and 2 loses I was offered a professional boxing contract. A promotor came to me after a match on Weed St. He gave his card to me. He'd seen me fight a few times, remembered where I fought, who I fought, and how I won.

"You're fighting anyway fellow. The crowds are paying, the

venues are making money off of you. Why not take the headgear off, fight pro, and actually get paid for what you're doing? I can get you five hundred a fight to start, and we'll move it up from there."

The carriage driving money was getting me by, regardless, an extra five hundred bucks once or twice a month wouldn't hurt. And why not? The promotor was right, I was fighting anyway, and the places I fought all made money on the tickets and the beer. Why shouldn't I get a cut of that?

"I'll tell you why." Joe said to me as he sat on the side of the ring. "You're white. That means you're valuable. You can sell fights. Listen to me kid, I've been in this game a long time, had this same talk with Darrius, Luke, and half a dozen others over the years. Stephan is a pro, you aren't."

"I don't see why not."

"Let me tell you what he's going to do to you. You'll win your first pro fight, you'll win it real easy. You know why? Because the guy you'll fight won't have a clue what he's doing. There's nothing stopping anyone from going pro. So you'll cut to 147 like you always do. Meanwhile he'll find a guy who actually weighs 147 to match you up against. That guy will likely never have boxed before in his life. Not in a single match, not in the gym, nothing. You're a good fighter, by the time the match starts you'll also be ten lbs bigger than he is. They'll pay him a hundred dollars to take a beating, and you'll beat the hell out of him. The ref will let it go longer then it should, because the crowd loves it. And why will the crowd love it? Because you're white, and the guy they match you up to give a beating to will be black.

Then they'll do it again, and you'll beat the hell out of some Mexican who doesn't know how to fight. Then you'll beat up a few more blacks who don't know nothing about boxing. Soon you'll be 4-0 as a pro. Then you'll be 7-0 as a pro.

Now you got a record. Now they can put you up as the co-main event, the Great White Hope. Doesn't matter that all seven of your pro fights were easier than any fight you've had as an amateur. You're seven and zero, that's all the crowd knows.

Now you'll be matched up against a killer. A black guy who's been boxing since he was four years old. A guy with a hundred and fifty amateur fights. Now you're there to pad his record, and he'll knock you out cold.

Now you're seven and one. Still a great record. And they'll do it to you again, put your white face on a poster against some black guy who's six and zero and call it a real match. But again, this guy has two hundred amateur matches and he'll kill you inside of a round.

Next they'll move you out of the city, and they'll put you up again, and you'll get knocked out again. It will keep happening until you've been knocked out five or more times in a row and they can't sell you anymore. Then, they'll dump you and go find another fool. That's the game."

I stood in the ring, listening, nodding.

"Listen to me kid. You won almost every amateur fight I put together for you. You did good, real good. You got those fast hands, and you got heart, but you're never going to be a fighter. I didn't get you young enough. And besides, you got too many options. You're funny, right?

"Yeah."

"So go be funny. And if that doesn't work, start a business. You're smart. Don't come back here anymore."

"Joe…"

"No I mean it. You're not going to be a pro, and you got nothing left to prove."

Joe looked across the gym to Mike, the old Italian actor who was hitting the heavy bag. "Hey Mike!" Mike stopped. "He looks like me, doesn't he? Good looking kid with a big nose."

"Yeah, he does."

"You know I never had a son." Mike returned to punching the bag. Joe turned back to me. "Go on kid, get out of here, don't come back."

And so, I didn't.

Chicago was an amazing town for amateur comedy. I averaged seven to ten sets a week. Meanwhile in New York guys had to hustle all day, standing out on the street corners and begging every passersby to come to their shows that night. If they could get five paying people into the club, then they would be allowed to perform. Other states, like my home state of Michigan, just didn't have that much opportunity for new comics. Guys were lucky if they could perform two or three times a week, no matter how dedicated they were.

After a long period of doing up to ten open mic sets per week, I was ready. I felt like a pro, and bookers were starting to agree.

"It's a four hundred seat club." I told Rylan excitedly as we ate fifty-nine cent tocos at one am.

I had an agent now. Maybe not the biggest or best agent, but she booked paid shows all over the Midwest, and she could use me as an opening act almost every weekend.

But I wasn't available every weekend. I had worked the phones, hustled, and called all the major clubs in Michigan, Illinois, Wisconsin, Indiana, and Ohio. Quite a few of them booked me.

This weekend, at a place called Trippers, I would be opening for a minor star, getting paid to do fifteen minutes of stage time in front of four hundred people.

"It's all bullshit man, you know that right, like none of it's real, your whole act sucks, you suck, this entire business sucks, I hate it here, I hate fifty-nine cent tacos, this restaurant sucks, this entire city sucks!"

Rylan walked out. We never called each other again. I saw him a few times at Chicago clubs, but he refused to say hello to me.

I sat in the green room of Tripper's Comedy Club in Lansing, Michigan. I had arrived early and counted chairs. Tonight would be a sold out show of four-hundred people.

Bobby Collins was headlining. He wasn't an A list star, but he wasn't some small club journeyman either. He'd had a long career, including spots on Leno and Letterman, toured with Frank

Sinatra, worked shows with Chris Rock, and performed at the White House. He was A minus, only one step down from the huge names.

I stared at his poster, impressed. But mostly I looked at the bottom right corner. There it was. "Also appearing, Joel Paul Reisig!". No bio, no picture, but I was on the poster!

As if reading my mind, I heard Bobby behind me, "You must be Also Appearing."

"That's me."

"Just have fun out there."

"How long do you want me to do?"

"Whatever you want. If you only have five, do five. If you can keep them rolling for fifteen or twenty, go ahead."

We shook hands and he stepped back out, back to his own (presumably even nicer) green room. I went back to staring at my name on the poster.

A waitress entered.

"Hi! Can I get you anything?"

"Um, iced tea?"

"Sure. Would you like some dinner waiting for you here when you get off stage?"

"Um…" I didn't really have any money.

"It's all free. Drinks too."

"Oh! Ah, they're bringing me up right now. You have steaks?"

"It will be waiting for you in fifteen minutes. Potatoes and veggies ok?"

"Yeah. I got to go!"

I heard my name, four hundred people clapped politely, and I stepped onto the bright stage.

I drove back to Chicago and packed my stuff. My lease was over. I had an agent for comedy now, and a schedule for the road, my need for Chicago's endless list of one-night amateur comedy rooms was over. But I had one more fight.

I met Gino downtown, in his gym. One of the assistant coaches let us in. "Pull the door shut when you leave, it will lock behind you."

The lights were dim, the gym empty, all eerily quiet. I couldn't leave Chicago without a tie breaker, and Gino couldn't let me. We had to know.

Gino stepped into the ring. "No headgear, eight-ounce fighting gloves."

I nodded.

"No rounds, no breaks."

I nodded again.

"And no matter what happens, it stays here. We never talk about it."

Gino and I came together in the center of a ring, for the third time.

Afterward:

After leaving Chicago I toured, professionally, as a standup comedian for roughly a year. When I say professionally, I mean that I was paid to do comedy. I wasn't paid much.

Gigs were generally Thursday night through Saturday night, with two shows on Friday and two shows on Saturday. I played at a lot of legit clubs around the Midwest, either as the opening act or sometimes as the middle (featured) act of a three-person show. On the road I was the opener for established comedians in their 40s through 70s.

I enjoyed being on stage. Always have.

I didn't enjoy checking into cheap motels, sitting around diners all day waiting for the sun to set, or the idea that I would one day turn into a 55-year-old headliner who is still playing cheap provincial clubs, alcoholic, on my third marriage, and being rejected by the waitresses.

If you read my book, *Midnight Run*, it starts with a breakup between myself and "Candise" (not her real name). On that day, I stopped being funny. And I stopped doing standup.

Years later I began to feel funny again, but standup was no longer for me. I continued in the film business and, obviously, writing books. I hope that you find them humorous.

I stepped back on stage about a year ago. I wrote an entirely new set, all about having young children. Nobody in the clubs knew me anymore. It was an amateur night, I dropped my name in the hat, got a number, and did a set. It was as if I had never stepped away. If anything, I was funnier than I used to be. My material now fit the age group of the audience.

I did not return. Maybe I will again, maybe I won't.

After touring for a full year, working with different professionals every weekend, I can confidently say that Rylan Worth was the funniest unknown comic I have ever seen perform. I have googled his real name many times, and never found any reference to him. I can only assume that he quit comedy years ago. He likely works at the fifty-nine-cent taco place, telling all the customers how much they suck.

I lost touch with Gino; I have not spoken to him in over a decade. I tried to find him a few times online, but he simply isn't there.

I do know that he turned pro shortly after I left Chicago, winning his first six fights. He was then brutely knocked out eight times in a row. His coach, his father, was gone, there was no one to protect him from the game.

Stephan Bonnar was inducted into the UFC Hall of Fame in 2013. Stephan retired from fighting, married, and had a son. He named his son Griffin, in honor of his rival and friend Forrest Griffin. When two men share a ring like they did, it changes you and bonds you forever.

ABOUT THE AUTHOR

Joel Paul Reisig

Former standup comedian turned author Joel Paul Reisig has worked as a wrangler, driven in a demolition derby, competed in the longest kayak race in the world, boxed in the Golden Gloves, ridden bulls and wrestled alligators, and raced a dog sled ninety miles across Michigan's frozen upper peninsula. He invites you to come on his next adventure with him, and promises you that you will laugh every step of the way.

BOOKS BY THIS AUTHOR

Inca Trail To Machu Picchu

Joel Paul Reisig, "our generation's Bill Bryson", takes you on a Peruvian adventure in the book that has been called "Seinfeld on the Inca Trail". This is the reality of what it is like to actually hike the pathways of the Incas exactly how they did six hundred years ago, assuming they had porters running ahead of them to set up their tents, cook their meals, clean their toilets, administer oxygen, remind them to put on sunscreen, and pose them for pictures. It is an account of sixteen first world tourists on a quest for social media photos. In between humorous anecdotes I will attempt to, quickly, slip in some history, local facts, and culture. Don't worry, you'll hardly feel it.

"Read it, loved it!" Richard Karn (Al, from the TV show Home Improvement)

Midnight Run

Amazon's #1 Bestseller in Kindle Humor!!! (top of list on 9/28/20)

"Authentic and funny. Joel nails a rookie's blunders and achievements on the trail with sled dogs"
-Jeff King, four-time Iditarod champion

In the hilarious new travelogue by Joel Paul Reisig, the author has a heart attack and is dumped by the women he loves. He decides to move to Michigan's frozen Upper Peninsula where he lives with an old musher, a moron, and forty-seven sled dogs, races in the Midnight Run, and falls for a girl who conveniently has the same name as the girl he lost!

I Just Want Dry Underpants: An Average Joel Enters The World's Longest Kayak Race

In the hilarious new travelogue from Joel Paul Reisig "our generations Bill Bryson", the standup comedian turned adventure travel writer heads to Missouri and enters the world's longest kayak race, 340 nonstop miles across the entire state! Over the course of 77 hours of racing, Joel meets The Tan Man, a women with purple hair, a pastor, an Army colonel, a beer guzzling moron, a man with a baboon's heart, an eighty year old river dog, a college professor, and other colorful characters all crazy enough to take part in the toughest ultra-marathon on water! Joel strives to bring you into the boat with him as he paddles for three plus days – learning, laughing, and hallucinating!